LISTEN TO THE CHILDREN

Annejet Campbell

LISTEN
TO THE
CHILDREN

Compiled by Annejet Campbell

GROSVENOR
LONDON MELBOURNE OTTAWA
WELLINGTON RICHMOND VA

First published 1979
2nd Impression 1980

2nd edition published 1987
GROSVENOR BOOKS,
54 Lyford Road, London, SW18 3JJ

21 Dorcas Street, South Melbourne
Victoria 3205, Australia

302/141 Somerset Street West,
Ottawa, Ontario K2P 2HI
Canada

PO Box 1834, Wellington,
New Zealand.

GROSVENOR USA
PO Box 8647,
Richmond, VA 23226.

US Trade Distributor:
M & B Fulfillment Service Inc.,
540 Barnum Avenue,
Bridgeport, Conn. 06608

Design: Blair Cummock
Cover Design: W Cameron Johnson

British Library Cataloguing in Publication Data
Listen to the children; Parents tell their stories – 2nd ed.
1. Parents and child – case studies
I. Campbell, Annejet
306.8′74   HQ755.85

ISBN 1–85239–006–9

Library of Congress Catalog
Pre-assigned Card Number: 87–81505

Phototypeset by Input Typesetting Ltd,
London SW19 8DR

Printed by Richard Clay Ltd, Bungay, Suffolk, England

Contents

Foreword

THE FAMILY IS STILL the most important institution in the world today, yet from Moscow to Miami the divorce statistics soar. The effects of this breakdown are felt in every sphere of society. The children are often the helpless victims. What can be done?

We don't have to stand by helplessly and let it happen. There is something practical we can do starting today. What is God's plan for you and your family and how can you find it? The theme that links the stories in this book is the experience that to listen to the voice of God inside us can be the start of a new way of living together.

In these pages parents tell how they tackled small problems in children which could have turned into big ones.

Parents of teenagers tell how they kept sane during these tumultous years and how they helped their kids to get off drugs and depression and find a purpose in life.

Of course not all the stories reflect credit upon the parents, or could be described as successes, but they suggest an approach which others may find helpful.

Is the highest function of the home simply to perpetuate life—or to create a way of life worth perpetuating? The family unit can become a source of power for transforming society.

An earlier version of this book was published in Britain in 1979, the International Year of the Child. It has been translated into six other languages including Chinese.

Told with remarkable frankness the stories in this book are all true. Only the names have been changed.

I would like to thank all those who gave their stories for

this book as well as those who spent many hours typing and heightening the manuscript.

Above all I am grateful to Paul and our daughters for their encouragement and for never hesitating to give me their honest opinions while I was working on this book.

ANNEJET CAMPBELL

Annejet, Digna, Edith Anne and Paul Campbell.

1 Listen to the children

MY HUSBAND Paul and I come from very different backgrounds. He was born on the Canadian prairies, the son of a Yorkshire mother and a Highland father who was a Scottish Baptist minister. I, on the other hand, am an industrialist's daughter from Holland, who grew up with my three brothers and three sisters in an occupied country, each of my parents being taken away to concentration camps at different times. What Paul's and my parents had in common was a strong faith in God, a faith which grew stronger through the hardships of the prairie and the dangers of the war.

Paul and I, each in our own way, lost much of this inheritance, and had each to find faith for ourselves, by which time he was a successful young doctor at the Henry Ford Hospital in Detroit and I was a rebellious twenty-year-old, learning French and fashion in Paris. It was the determination to try and bring that faith into the affairs of individuals and nations which contrived our meeting and later, in 1957, our marriage. We now live in London and have two daughters, Edith Anne and Digna, in their early twenties.

It is with them that this book begins. When they were a lot younger, I asked them some questions.

What, I asked, do they feel when Paul and I don't or won't listen to their ideas? Their answers were clear and incisive:

- It makes me not want to do anything you ask me to do.
- It makes me want to smash plates to get your attention, especially when we have guests.
- I feel neglected.
- I feel my ideas don't count.

- I want to run away from home.

How do you feel if we do listen to you?
- I feel secure.
- I feel I can talk to you about anything.
- Life is not a strain.
- I feel I can be myself.

Why do you think some parents don't listen?
- They are too wrapped up in themselves.
- They feel superior, they think they know better.
- They are afraid their kids will come out with something they can't handle.
- They don't want to spare the time.
- They don't care.

What sort of world do you want to see?
- Where everyone is free.
- Where everyone has enough food, a home and work.
- No wars.
- There should be no bloodshed, but solving conflicts by talking together.
- You have to have certain laws; if everyone does their own thing you will have chaos.
- Families should be secure, happy units, no divorce.
- All children should have an equal chance to go to school.
- There should be no discrimination of colour anywhere.

Is this a picture of the kind of world we owe to our children? After all, they were born as a result of our actions and decisions and yet they inherit the mess we create.

The following are a few stories of what can happen if we take seriously what our children are trying to tell us. The first one comes from a friend who lives in Cape Town, South Africa.

Our two young daughters are quite different in character. Clare, now eight, is a quiet, reflective girl, very much aware of her dignity. She is cautious and likes to be sure she knows all the facts before taking any action.

Vicky, three years younger, is extrovert, a non-stop bundle of energy. You have only to see her, barely able to swim, plunge delightedly into the deep end of the swimming pool to sense her approach to life.

In our family all the jealousies and competition which are normal between any two children have arisen. Last year Clare suddenly burst out, 'Mummy, I hate Vicky. Couldn't we swap her for another baby?'

My first reaction was to say, 'Oh no, you don't really hate her,' and to try to smooth it over. Then I thought, 'That isn't right. Accept that if Clare says she hates, then she does.'

I waited for a few days until the subject came up again. Then I told Clare how at times when I was growing up I had hated my brother.

'Did you really, Mummy? What did you do?'

So I told her how I had decided to say sorry to my brother for my jealousy and how, bit by bit, we had become good friends. I said how important it was for us to learn to change hate into caring, otherwise what could we do about the fighting in Ireland or the divisions in South Africa—both of which countries we have lived in?

Nothing dramatic happened, but Clare got the point. A couple of weeks later she said to me, 'You know, I like Vicky a little better now.' And most of the time they are good friends.

One afternoon when my younger daughter Digna was six or seven, she came home from school saying, 'I don't want to go to school tomorrow. I don't like it any more.' I made no comment. A while later I suggested she might make a list of the things she did not like in school. She took a piece of paper and wrote down five points:

It is noisy.
I am shy.
I get tired.
It's a bit boring.
I have no one to play with at playtime.

The last point seemed to be the real bottleneck. We talked about it a bit, and I suggested that next day at playtime she might look around to see if there were any other girls looking lost and lonely with whom she could be friends. The next morning she left for school without complaints, and from then on gradually began to enjoy school and make a lot of friends.

Then there is the story sent to me by a Canadian friend who has done a series of television programmes on family life in her city.

My daughter Ellen, who was four at the time, saw the photo of her Daddy, who had been away for longish periods in connection with his work, and said, 'Hello, Daddy,' and then began to whine and sulk, demanding, 'When is my Daddy coming home?'

I knew I could do one of three things: cry with her as I was missing him too, be cross and send her to her room, or try an experiment.

I said to Ellen, 'Would you like to tell Jesus about it?'

She hesitated, then replied, 'Yes, I will.' She knelt down all by herself and said, 'Dear Jesus, I do want my Daddy to come home because I love him so much. Bye bye, Jesus.'

Her face was shining and she told me, 'Do you know what Jesus said to me? He said Daddy had to be away a little longer, then he was coming home to see me,' and she went off singing.

Often we feel superior to our children and disregard their suggestions as being impractical or plain stupid. But they may be right.

A French friend told me of her experience:

When our second son was three months old, he used to get into a terrible state every afternoon around six and could not stop crying. We didn't know what to do. One evening at the dinner table I suggested that we should listen to the little voice inside to see what to do.

Our eldest son, then six, thought we ought to go and sing a particular song to his brother. We thought that solution rather too simple, but we stood around the cradle and sang. The baby stopped crying and went to sleep. Since then we have always sung that song to the child before he goes to sleep. Curiously, it marked the end of evening crying.

4

A farmer's wife from New Zealand writes:

We had a 'problem child'—a baby girl who never ate if she could avoid it. Every meal became a battle and it went on for three years, during which I tried everything! At my wits' end, I was challenged to ask God to show me the answer. As I sat quietly, I remembered the resentment I had felt at the conception of this child. I had pushed this feeling down, out of sight, as unworthy of a 'Christian mother', and completely forgotten it after her birth. Now it was as if God put His finger on that resentment deep in my heart. When the child was difficult, I became hard. It came from that core of resentment. That was our problem.

When I saw what it had done to her, I could only weep, and repent, and I was cleansed and forgiven. When I obeyed the simple directions God gave me—never again to force her to eat—the problem was solved overnight. She never again refused to eat.

Sometimes we talk too much when we should really be trying to create the atmosphere in which a child can listen to his own conscience. A mother of four, who lives in Holland, sent me this story:

Our youngest son Tom, twelve years old, came home from school at lunchtime looking a bit pale. He said, 'This afternoon is the school sports day, but I am not going because I have a lot of homework and I'm too tired.'

He could not stay away without my permission and I felt I should not give it—but I was not really sure. I went into the kitchen. Tom came in to persuade me to agree.

I said, 'Let's sit down for a minute and not talk—just think.'

My only conclusion was, 'Let him decide for himself.'

After half a minute he jumped up, saying, 'If I run fast I can still make it,' and he rushed out of the door.

We often want to shield our children from unpleasant situations. An English friend told me her experience:

My daughter, Phoebe, is an only child, now seven years old. In the last year two friends of her age had a baby brother and a baby sister. 'I want a baby brother or sister—I think I'd rather have a sister,' was her constant plea. And she kept looking hopefully to see if I was getting any larger. I tried to avoid the issue, giving her vague replies. But I knew we would not be having another child.

We went to stay with a friend for a few days and I talked to her about this. 'Should you go on keeping her in suspense?' she asked.

I thought about it and decided to talk to Phoebe openly when the right opportunity came. Soon we were walking together by the sea and I said to her, 'You know, Daddy and I would love to give you a baby brother or sister, but I'm afraid we can't.' I told her about a baby I had lost before she was born and she asked various questions.

As we got back to the house, she suddenly said, 'Why did you have to tell me?' She ran to her room and I found her in floods of tears on the bed. My heart sank and I wondered if I had done the wrong thing. She came to lunch still rather tearful. But after a while she cheered up and became very outgoing to our hostess. She was like a different child.

That afternoon she was invited out to tea with a neighbouring family. In her bath that evening Phoebe said to me, 'I told Mrs X all about your not being able to have another baby.'

'My heavens,' I thought, 'what has she been saying?'

'And,' went on Phoebe, 'she said that she lost two babies too.'

I, too, stopped feeling she was deprived in some way, and started to be grateful for what we do have. I have a sister but come from a broken home. My father left home when I was eight. This background, I think, can be much more damaging for a child. As an only child, Phoebe has had to make the effort to go out to make friends. We have lived abroad and moved about quite a bit, so she has had the opportunity to make some very good friendships.

Another friend writes of how her son overcame his fear of being bullied at school:

Nicky was six years old. He liked school. There was only one snag; every afternoon a big boy of ten would rush out of school after him. Nicky would try to run away but Peter would catch up and start tripping him, throwing his cap in the pond, and so on. Nicky was frightened of this boy. I offered to fetch him from school, but he thought this was babyish.

At bedtime one night he asked Jesus what to do. Suddenly his face was radiant and he said, 'Jesus said that dogs run after cats because the cats are frightened and run away as fast as they can. So tomorrow I mustn't run but wait for Peter and walk home with him and try to make friends with him because he hasn't any.'

The next afternoon I looked out of the window and there they were, like a couple of old buddies, walking home together and stopping at our gate to finish their conversation. Gradually Nicky's friends also became Peter's friends.

An English headmaster told a friend of mine, 'Parents give their children everything except time.' A mother writes from Scotland:

When children are small the mother has to spend a good deal of time with them. As they grow up and can do things for themselves both parent and child can enjoy the independence this brings. But it is still important to give enough time to listen to the things my boys want to talk about. The best time is often when they are going to bed and can chat in a relaxed way. Sometimes it takes a real effort to go upstairs— I am tired at the end of the day and feel I have a right to relax!

One evening my elder son was comparing how much pocket money his friends got with what we were giving him. He found he came off very badly! Then he said, 'Of course I would like to have more pocket money, but you and Dad

teach us to listen to God and that is much more important.' After a pause he told me about a friend who got what he thought was a phenomenal amount and added, 'You know, I think his parents give him so much money to make up for what they don't give him.'

This point is also illustrated by a Swiss friend who has worked with children of all nationalities.

One thing I have noticed: parents often promise material things to children with the idea that it will make them happy. But when I asked some eight-year-old boys what made them happy, none of them mentioned anything material. Their answers were:

Doing something really difficult.

Helping someone who really needs it.

And when I asked them whether they were happy when they got what they wanted, an Irish boy answered, 'When I get *all* I want, I don't get happy, I get greedy.'

My Swiss friend put a number of questions to a group of children from seven different countries between the ages of seven and thirteen. Here are some of their answers:

What is your idea of an ideal family?
- A family where nobody tells lies. Where they don't fight, the way Mum and Dad do sometimes.
- Where we see more of Dad, at least at meal times. It would be good if parents would work less so that we could talk to them when we need them.
- Where parents would let us do things for ourselves. If they just give orders we become like robots who learn nothing.

What can children do to change the atmosphere at home?
- Tell the truth.
- Admit when we are wrong.
- We could say sorry.
- Everyone makes so much noise in our family that Mother gets angry. If we were quieter she would not get so angry.

- Have more times of listening to God together.

What sort of things do you quarrel about?
- Only little things, but they seem to let off fireworks and then they become big things.
- If my brother or sister has something that I don't have, I get jealous.
- If the parents say no to one child and yes to the other.

How could your family help other families?
- By telling them the things we think about in our home.
- By meeting our neighbours.
- We have to be united ourselves first before we can help others.

What sort of things do you like to do with your family?
- Go on holidays.
- Talk together about all sorts of things.
- Go to the woods.
- Play table tennis with Dad.

How do you make decisions in your family?
- We don't.
- Each one takes a notebook and writes down what he would like to do.
- We decide in the evening before saying our prayers.
- Everyone gives their ideas and Dad decides what is best.

Why do we need families?
- Because we need to eat.
- To look after us.
- We need a father to bring us up and show us how to live.

What are grandparents for?
- A grandmother is a lady who has no children of her own and therefore she loves other people's little boys and girls.
- Grandmothers don't do anything, they just need to be there. They never say, 'Come quickly,' or, 'Hurry up, for heaven's sake.'
- They are fat, but not too fat to do up our shoelaces. They wear glasses and sometimes they are able to pull out your tooth.
- They know the answers to questions like 'Why dogs hate

cats' and 'Why isn't God married?'

- When they read us a story they never skip any pages and they don't mind if it is always the same story.
- Everybody should have a grandmother, especially if you don't have television.
- Grandmothers are the only grown-ups who always have time for you.
- Grandma always thinks of us and telephones us. She always plays games with us. Grandmothers have their

limits, they send us to bed and don't give us any sweets before supper.

- Grandfathers have no limits, they just want us to have a good time.
- They see to it that our mothers behave themselves.

What does listening to God mean to a child? I asked Digna to give her explanation.

You sit quietly and you don't think about anything really, you just sit there and let your conscience roll, if you know what I mean. You don't hear a strange voice. I guess God is using your own voice to tell you something, and you can tell whether it's the devil or God speaking, because God says good things or where you've been wrong, and the devil says, 'Oh, forget it, you don't need to listen to Him.'

I was staying with a friend and one night we were talking in bed about eleven o'clock and God cropped up in our

conversation, and I asked my friend if she believed in Him, and she said, 'I think so, I'm not sure.'

I asked, 'When you've had a row with your mother, do you hear a little voice inside you saying, "Go and say sorry?" ' and she said, 'Yes, I had a big row the other day and I said to myself, "I will not say sorry"—but then a voice inside me said, "You must say sorry," and I did, and I was so happy.'

To a child, listening to the voice in your heart comes very naturally. It is not a new idea, of course—in the Bible there are countless stories of God giving instructions to people. When kings and leaders obeyed those instructions all went well in their lands, but when they chose to disregard God famine, war and chaos followed. I believe it is still so today.

2 Tackling problems together

AT A WORKSHOP on family life in Germany recently, the question was put:

At what age should you start saying 'no' to your child?

A German mother replied, 'As early as possible. You have to start setting limits when the children are very young. This gives them a sense of security and safety. Experiments with anti-authoritarian education have shown how disastrous it is if you don't do this. If you do establish certain limits it increases the so-called frustration-tolerance: the child learns that the world does not fall apart if he does not get his way. I sometimes meet children who have never heard "no" consistently. They have always been able to get their way by coaxing or coercion. We need to show a positive kind of authority.'

In this chapter parents tell how they have tackled small problems in children which could turn into big problems if not dealt with at an early age.

The first story is written by an English mother who teaches and has three young children.

I knew about praying, but the listening part was where the reality of God became evident. We need to treat it as an art. In the face of family quarrels, sickness, tiredness, pressures, there is always the way out. If we are willing to hear, God will speak to us in the most secret place of our hearts.

Since I began to listen, there have been changes in our family life. I had felt a kind of restless unease about my eldest daughter, aged six. She had become very clinging and was constantly demanding my attention. I resorted to a secret plea to God, not really expecting any answer. However, as I was standing there in the supermarket queue a thought came. It was that I was academically ambitious for my daughter, and was causing her anxiety which it was unfair for her to have to bear. As I recognised this thought as an answer, the burden lifted.

When I got home I explained to her, as best I could, how I had been wrong to expect too much of her and how sorry I was if she had felt I was pushing her. Her relief was pathetic. She did understand. Since then I have had a real change of heart towards her, and as a result her attitude towards school work has become much more careful and cheerful. She stopped copying other children, because she felt free to be herself, without having to live up to what I had wrongly expected of her.

Children seem to know at an early age that we all have two voices speaking in our hearts: a good one and a bad one. Once Edith Anne, then almost four, said to a friend who was visiting us, 'I'll tell you all that is in my heart. There is Jesus and there is the devil who wants to make everybody unhappy. You have to say to him, "I'm not going to listen to you."'

One evening, some time after that, she was in an exasperating mood, whining and fussing about everything. The following morning she said to me, 'I'm not going to whine again like I did last night.'

I asked, 'Why were you so naughty?'

She replied, 'I had a devil in me, but I shooted him.'

A young Cambodian couple, who now live in Paris, had a similar experience with their six-year-old son. Both their families have had political positions in their country and they carry on their hearts the terrible agonies suffered by their people.

About six months ago, my husband and I realised that our way of life was not right. We decided to stop thinking only about ourselves. We started to live for our son who is six (who had suffered a lot from our disunity), for each other, and for other men and women who need us.

16

Then together we tried to think about our son's education. We decided to be firm with him when necessary. We spend a certain amount of time each day talking and playing with him. (Both of us have jobs outside the home.) By giving this time to him quietly and regularly, he gets the security which I believe is needed for harmonious development of soul and character.

Our son has noticed the change in us. When he sees that we are about to start an argument, he says, 'Maman, Papa, would you like to listen to God?'

He is still young and our experience of change is new, but I have confidence in the future. Children are often much more aware than parents realise. One night our son was misbehaving at bedtime when suddenly he reappeared and said, 'Maman, my bad voice told me to go under the bed, but I told him, "Go away, bad voice. I will not listen to you. I will listen to the good voice who tells me not to disobey my mother." ' He understood the choice between good and bad. I hope that as he grows up this capacity for discernment will grow.

I once knew a teenager who would eat nothing but sausages and French fries. We decided early on that our children should learn to eat everything, and not waste food in an age where many are starving. We would give them a very small helping of things they did not like and after some time they would eat them without fuss and begin to like them.

A small girl of three stayed with us for some weeks. She was not used to finishing all the food on her plate. We told her that in our house everybody did. At first she was angry; but she responded when she saw we were firm. After every meal she would say triumphantly, 'I ate all my macaroni!' (or whatever it was). Children are eager to extend their capabilities, and we fail them if we do not help them do what they know to be right.

When Digna was four, she could not sit through a meal without getting off her chair several times with lots of excuses. My threats had no effect and meals turned into battle-fields. We decided to put a stop to this. We hung a chart on the wall. After every meal when she had not got up once she was allowed to stick a red paper star on the chart. If, on Saturday, she had seven times three stars on the chart, we would go and buy an ice-cream. It became a game to win a star after every meal. After several weeks, Digna forgot about the stars, but sitting all through the meal had become a firm habit. I suppose that children can learn good habits just as simply as they can pick up bad ones.

A Canadian friend sends another experience:

Having felt unhappy about the children's table manners for a while, I finally decided to give it serious thought. It struck me quite forcefully that my laziness in serving quick meals around the kitchen table was encouraging the children's bad manners. So I decided to make the extra effort of having family meals in the dining-room. The change has been quite remarkable. The children have to set and clear the table, which gives them a sense of responsibility. Evening meals are now fun and a chance for everyone to tell about their day.

This year my husband has insisted that the children, six

and four, make their beds, and on Saturday morning each one has to clean his room, which includes vacuuming. At the beginning it was a real struggle to get them to do it. Last Saturday, Harry was away on business and I was out teaching. When we got back the baby-sitter told us the children had insisted on cleaning their rooms all on their own. They now take great pride in showing off their well-made beds and tidy rooms.

And then there is this story from an American mother:

Our three elder boys left home when Tim was about seven—so he became like an only child. One of the problems in so many American homes is mother controlling things instead of respecting father's rightful place, as God ordained it, to be the head of the home. Well, I was in control with Tim. When Dick, my husband, would want to discipline him, I would protect Tim or be soft. I couldn't figure why Dick would be overly cross with the boy, unreasonably so, I thought.

I had recently learned to turn to God for answers when things were not right, and to see where I just might be wrong myself. My answer was, 'Dick wasn't mad at Tim, but at me.' I told this to Dick, and he said, 'That's true.'

After that, when Dick disciplined Tim, even if I felt it wasn't fair or that he was overly strict, I kept out of it, and backed Dick. Tim then couldn't turn to me for my softness. The results were that Tim was more secure, and he and Dick became close friends and it holds the same today.

Since then I've seen how so many children play one parent against the other. I am grateful that we learned to listen to God, and to find the unity that strengthened our family and gave us a faith. Our sons are now in the world as responsible citizens—with a concern for mankind and the country.

Some years ago Karen and her parents stayed with us for a few days on their way home to Los Angeles. Both parents did post-graduate work in Oxford, and her father was an All-American football player. Her mother writes:

I have found that whatever the problem with the kids, once I make up my mind to be firm about a particular thing they sense it before I even have a chance to do anything. For example, Karen, four years old, had been taking my make-up and jewellery for weeks—sometimes hiding it in her dresser drawer, sometimes using it when I wasn't looking. I felt it was very important that she learnt to respect other people's belongings. So I decided to give her her own jewellery and some old make-up things, including an eyebrow brush, which she could keep next to mine.

She was not allowed in my bedroom when I wasn't there. I was prepared to put a latch on my door if necessary, but as soon as I had decided on this plan of action, she stopped taking my things. It was as if she sensed that I really meant it, and wasn't going to try to play games about it.

When our children got into moods I used to say to them, 'If you want to be moody, go to your room. If you decide to be cheerful then we like having you with us.' Invariably they would prefer the family circle to voluntary confinement. They realised that they could often decide themselves to snap out of it and need not be helpless victims of moods. Of course, some moods had a deeper cause, and then we had to find out what it was.

Digna, who was delivered by a very competent midwife, had a habit of falling asleep while she should be feeding. The midwife showed me various ways of waking her up.

'As soon as the cord is cut they will try to control you,' she said. 'You must decide who is going to be in charge!'

Edith Anne was four and used to have terrible temper tantrums. She would lie on the floor and kick and scream every time she didn't get what she wanted. I often gave in for the sake of peace.

A friend said, 'It is bad for the child to feel she can control you. How are you going to help her?'

We had no idea. We decided to ask for God's help, as we realised it was no good picking on every point that was wrong. It made life unbearable for all concerned. We got the thought to insist on three simple points of behaviour:

She must make her bed and tidy her room every morning before breakfast.

She must finish all the food on her plate.

She must be told what to wear and not change her clothes without consent.

And there was a fourth point, for me: not to avoid crossing her will even if a volcano might erupt.

We told Edith Anne our decisions on the three points. She made no comment. The next morning I discovered a terrible mess in her room. I told her to tidy it up before coming down. In less than a minute she was down. I said, 'Did you tidy your room?' She said, 'Yes, but don't go and look now . . . !' Actually, we did go up and tidied the room quickly together.

As we insisted on these points, she became a much happier child. The tantrums almost totally disappeared. It gave her a sense of security to know what was expected of her and how far she could go. I think she knew that I was no longer afraid of crossing her will, and the storms seemed to subside before they had a chance to erupt. She also knew that Paul and I *were united, so she couldn't play one against the other. You know what little girls are like with their fathers!*

Still, this business of saying 'no' I always find hard. I suppose it is because I am a coward. Some years later when Edith Anne was about eight, she wanted to do something, I can't remember what, but I felt I should say 'no'. I was dreading it and that evening as I was clearing up the kitchen I found myself having a conversation with the Almighty; I said to Him, 'Do I really have to go on crossing this girl's will for ever and ever? I am tired of it. Can't I just give in now and then for the sake of peace?' The reply came right away, 'Instead of dreading it, you should be grateful for every chance you get to cross her will, because she has a very strong one and if you don't cross it for her while she is small, she won't let Me do it when she is big.'

This was a new way of looking at it, a new perspective. Of course our children don't belong to us, they belong to God and if they are to be His instruments, then obedience to His will is perhaps most important. I saw that as parents we can help prepare them for this when they are small.

After that evening, whenever I knew I was going to have to say 'no' to her I would say to myself, 'O.K. boys, here we go again, it's all for the future. . . .'

Fortunately, losing her temper became a thing of the past.

A French friend, who lives in Lyon, has two lively sons:

It was one of those evenings when a mother is at the end of her tether, having to cope with a dozen things at a time, when children are tired and excited. My nine-year-old son was having a bath and being very naughty. I came in and spanked him and shouted, 'I could kill you, I could kill you!' As soon as I had said it, I felt very ashamed.

Later on, at bedtime, I felt I could not let him go to sleep without putting things right. I did not feel I should apologise, because his behaviour had been wrong, but I asked him, 'What did you feel when I told you that very nasty thing?'

He answered very shyly, 'Oh Mummy, I often think that about you, but I don't dare say it!' We laughed together and felt very alike and close to each other.

22

I had to face the fact that with incidents like that it is only my real nature which comes out, and not that of the wonderful mother who takes such good care of her children.

I went on thinking about it, wondering what more there was besides tiredness which made me act like that. It occurred to me that when for some reason (usually a very specific one) I am not letting God control my life, I immediately start trying to control my family. My son told me once, 'Mummy, you sometimes act like a queen around here.' He was right, and it was no compliment!

Another mother writes from California:

The other day our ten-year-old son and some of his friends found some *Penthouse* magazines in a neighbour's trash can. Of course they thought it was very exciting and they all came into John's room, closed the door and leafed through all the pictures. Then they hid them, and it was to be their secret.

However, that night John obviously had something on his mind, but said he couldn't tell because he had promised the others not to.

I said, 'Knowing you, something is bothering you and you won't be happy until you can tell me or Dad about it. We can keep secrets.'

He did, with great embarrassment, and we had a good talk. His Dad had had a 'facts of life' talk with him much earlier, so he knew he could discuss everything with us. God has a wonderful purpose for sex, just as He does for food, but you can get awfully sick from eating too much food (especially chocolate!), just as you can misuse sex.

We made an agreement—he would tell his friends that we would take the magazines to sell for recycled paper and divide the money. He convinced his friends that this was a good deal.

Mothers have feelings too. Edith Anne had been having piano lessons since she was eight, at her own request. She enjoyed playing but not practising. One afternoon, shortly before her twelfth birthday, I sat with her at the piano trying to encourage her to practise. I was a total failure. The more I

23

urged her to play, the more she resisted. We got into an argument. Nothing I said made any impact.

Finally I didn't know what to say any more. I felt utterly helpless and defeated, and I began to cry. I don't think I had ever cried in front of Edith Anne. There was a deadly silence. She was stunned. After a while I said, 'Daddy and I try to give you a good education, we try to give you what you need without spoiling you, but we must have failed somewhere.'

She flung her arms around me, sobbing, 'It's not your fault. I'm so selfish and ungrateful. Please forgive me.' Since that day our relationship has been totally different; we seem to be operating on the same wave-length instead of pulling in different directions.

A friend from Kenya writes about her young son going for the first time to boarding school.

Frank has known for a long time that he would be going to boarding school, and this year the plan materialised. We chose the same school his father went to when he was a boy. Frank is only seven and a half, and it seemed a very young age for him to be away from home. We had prepared him for it by talking about it quite often, so he knew a little of what it was all about, but of course when the moment came it was hard for him and for us, the more so as he had never spent a night away from his parents.

We took him to school one evening in September and hoped for the best, believing we had made the right decision, but with some doubts and apprehensions. After two weeks we had the opportunity to visit him at the school. We were amazed at the change in him. He had matured and grown up in a very short time. He showed us his work and where everything was, taking a real interest and pride in keeping his possessions in order. It had been hard for him to look after himself—to know, for instance, that the way you leave the clothes you take off in the evening is the way you find them the next morning. His letters were also cheerful, enquiring after all the members of the household.

After five weeks of school the time came for the four-day

half-term holiday. He appreciated everything so much more after being away—his toys, his bike and his food. Naturally he didn't want to go back, but he knew that he had to, and although there were tears he was brave again.

I myself noticed how much I wanted to keep him with me and thought that we, his parents, were the only ones who could do the best for him. And then suddenly you have no more control, and wonder if everything is going right. Then my husband said to me, 'God looks after him too, you know.'

How can a parent cope when suddenly left alone with young children? An English friend writes:

My daughter was only seven and my son four when my husband died suddenly. At first I did not see how I could face life without him. He was such a wonderful father and husband. But something in God's love for us as a family, and my husband's faith, gave me the courage to accept this as God's will and an experience of the Cross.

I was having serious problems with my daughter, Diana, who was reacting strongly against me. I could see no reason why she constantly hit out at me and I put it down to her missing her father, as they had been very close. One day the children at the school which both attended took part in a musical. They sang several songs in the play and had a few speaking lines, and all enjoyed it very much. At the final curtain the children sat in front of the footlights with their backs to the audience, watching the chorus sing the final song.

The first night as the audience applauded most of the children turned round and smiled at the audience. It was explained to them that they had had their applause earlier, and this was for the whole cast and it distracted attention if they turned round. The second night only Diana turned round. The producer was cross. A grown-up looking after Diana said to her, 'I think you should think about why you turned round.'

The children in the school used to take time regularly to listen to God, and the following morning, when they started

the day with a few minutes' sitting quietly, my daughter made no reference to the play but said, 'I am jealous of my brother. I don't know what to do.'

One of the teachers suggested she might like to talk to me about it. She did this, with great difficulty, and also said that she felt I liked her brother, John, better than her. I found it hard to accept that I could be guilty of something so unfair, but when I thought about it I knew that I was having to make increasing efforts to try to be patient with her, as she got more and more rebellious. John in the meantime was exploiting the situation and being sweet—and smug—as he saw his sister getting up against me.

It was a turning point in the security of both children, as Diana knew there was a higher authority to which we could always turn. It gave John security as he was getting very spoilt and correspondingly insecure.

An Australian journalist wrote of this experience with his son.

On the football field he was fearless. Yet every night sucking his thumb was an essential part of going to sleep. Andrew was nine years old and despite the earnest, even frantic efforts of my wife and me, there seemed to be no end to the habit.

We had tried painting his thumb with unpleasant tinctures, and sewing up his pyjama sleeves, but we realised the direct assault seemed merely to lead to a fruitless struggle of wills—ours against his.

Some weeks later I was kneeling by his bed about to say prayers with him when I found myself saying, to my surprise, 'Have you ever asked Jesus to help you stop sucking your thumb?'

I can still feel the penetrating look in his eyes as he answered, 'Jesus may work for you; He doesn't for me.'

'I don't find it all that easy myself,' I responded. 'Every day I have to ask for His help on something I can't do myself.'

'What was it today?' was the next question, with a definite emphasis on the 'today'.

Quick as a flash I remembered, and rather wished I hadn't. A debate went on inside me. It was not an example that would be helpful to him. In fact it might be harmful. Yet we had always made a rule to be completely honest in our replies to genuine questions—and there was no doubting the searching interest of Andrew at this point as his eyes levelled unblinkingly on mine.

'Well, as a matter of fact I had to ask Jesus's help not to look back at a picture on the cover of a magazine.'

'What was wrong with the picture?'

'It was dirty.'

The final question, 'And *did* you look again?' was answered by a rather relieved, 'No.'

Then he prayed. I don't remember the phrasing of his request for help. What I do remember is that he never sucked his thumb again.

Many years later Andrew told us that what had helped him most was that we were prepared to be dead honest with him about our needs, whether he volunteered anything or not.

An English woman doctor felt frustrated and defeated by the temperament of her small daughter.

Life was very pleasant and without problems until the children began to become little personalities with wills of their own, which I could no longer control. I found Lucy, our second daughter, the most difficult. There was just a year between her and the next one. She used to follow me from room to room crawling and crying, which was very irritating. At times I picked her up and shook her to stop her crying. It didn't work, of course, as I knew it wouldn't, but though I felt guilty afterwards I couldn't help myself.

By the time she was three she had begun to have real temper tantrums, including one occasion when she lay down on a shop floor and screamed. I never took her shopping again.

I felt angry about all this—here was I, a sensible, intelligent doctor, yet I could not handle my own daughter. I was defeated by a small child. Things got steadily worse, until one night in desperation I went down on my knees (a thing I was not at all in the habit of doing—we rarely went to church, or took any notice of God at that time). I said, 'O God, what am I to do with this child?'

The immediate thought came to me, as clearly as if spoken aloud, 'You know perfectly well what to do. You must start listening to Me again.'

So I did. I had been brought up to believe in the value of time spent first thing in the morning with God, and I decided to get up half an hour earlier to do this. It was quite a struggle as I met a lot of opposition from my husband. But fairly quickly I began to see a difference in all the children. It was not the children who were wrong, but me. I also found that I seemed to be able to get through a lot more in the day, and so I had more time to give to the children. Our relationships got better and better.

And, as an added gift, my husband decided to join me in the time of quiet in the morning.

When our third daughter, Elisabeth, was twelve, she began to be very difficult. A barrier was growing up between us.

28

She was keen on wild flowers, and one morning I had the idea to spend time with her collecting and pressing wild flowers. This didn't interest me in the least, and I didn't want to do it. But we began to go for walks, sometimes alone, sometimes with all the girls, when we would see who could find the greatest number of different ones. Elisabeth soon had a big scrap-book of pressed flowers—and what was more important, she and I became close to each other again.

What to do with a child who won't go to sleep?

A young couple in the west of England were very worried about their three-year-old daughter who did not want to go to sleep at night. The husband, Gordon, was working at the radio station which meant he often had to work late at night.

When he would see little Hannah still running around at 10. 30 in the evening he would start blaming his wife: 'You are some mother! You can't even keep control of your own child.' Martha was beginning to get desperate as well as exhausted from this hyper-active child who did not let up during the day either. Also the never-ending arguments with Gordon were getting her down.

A friend came to coffee one day and she gave Martha a copy of the first edition of this book. Martha read some of the stories and thought she might try the idea of listening to the voice of God in her heart. She had tried everything else and there was nothing to lose.

When she sat quietly trying to concentrate, suddenly an idea popped into her head: 'Tonight when Gordon comes home and he starts arguing, *don't* argue back.'

Gordon came home, late, looking tired. Seeing that Hannah was still up he started his usual flow of accusations. Martha did not say a word. Gordon looked at her and said, 'What's the matter with you? You ill or something?'

'I have been really worried about Hannah and about us and so I tried an experiment,' said Martha and she told him about it. For the first time in a long while they began to talk sensibly with one another, about Hannah and their feelings of inadequacy and their own relationship. They began to try the listening experience together every day. Soon Hannah, sensing the change of atmosphere in the house, became more peaceful and started to sleep more. That was the beginning of a change which is still going on.

Bed-wetting is a problem in many families. A Canadian mother writes:

When our eldest son, Jimmy, was four years old and still wetting his bed every night I took him to the doctor to find out what was wrong.

The doctor said to me, 'Now is the time to get him over it; if not he may never get over the problem. Did you know that grown men have to be discharged from the army for this kind of complaint?

I had never heard of such a thing. Without realising it I tucked a deep fear down in my heart about it.

I then made every effort to deal with what I thought was the problem, trying to restrict his fluids, and getting him up at night, sometimes several times in one night. The harder I tried the worse it got.

This went on for many years. I remember thinking Jimmy would never be able to leave home and I would spend the rest of my life washing bed linen.

Earlier in my life I had learned to listen to God, but somehow I had let the habit slip. One year at Easter I was inspired to begin all over again and I decided to let God run my life. Jimmy was thirteen by that time.

I began to get up earlier every morning to have a quiet time before my busy day started. We now had four children.

One morning the thought came very clearly, 'Jimmy will not get over his bed-wetting until you get over your fear about it.' Immediately I realised my unconscious fear I was able to give it to God, not that it didn't come back many times but each time I was tempted to let it in I would give it back again. I can remember literally pushing it out of my mind and saying sometimes out loud, 'God, I promised to give it up.'

I said to Jimmy, 'I have made a mess of my life and yours,

and I am sorry, but no longer am I going to take any responsibility for your bed-wetting. From now on it's up to you.'

He looked at me with a quizzical look on his face but didn't say anything. He knew I meant it. Almost immediately he began to improve and very shortly he was over it altogether. That summer he was able to go to camp for the first time.

When my husband and I went to his school in the fall, one teacher said, 'What has happened to Jimmy? He is a different boy.'

Now he is grown up and a medical doctor. I am convinced that when we as parents pay a price, such as getting up earlier and obeying that inner voice, miracles do happen.

Surveys show that adopted children, however well cared for by their new parents, often still feel neglected and grow up with a chip on their shoulder.

A friend in Yorkshire tells how she helped her children:

We have two adopted children, Jenny and Michael.

Spending a morning with a young Indian mother and her small baby, watching a baby being breast-fed for the first time, Jenny, aged seven, commented, 'I think I was fed like that for the first three weeks of my life.' Then followed a discussion on the merits of breast-feeding and bottle-feeding. Jenny said, 'I was born to a schoolgirl, you know.' The Indian woman was struck by her freedom to talk in this way without any sense of hold-back or self-consciousness.

Jenny was three when she had first asked me about herself as a baby. I told her the story of how we met her the first time. How she stayed asleep the whole time we held her, how we brought her home to live with us the next day and how happy we were to have a little daughter, because we hadn't been able to have any children of our own until then. Jenny asked me to tell her this 'story' on and off for some weeks. She didn't ask me much about what happened before she was six weeks old, although the fact of her growing in 'another lady's tummy' was talked about.

One Sunday when Jenny was six, she and Michael were

having a very happy game pretending I was their baby, ministering to all my needs. All I had to do was make the occasional pretend cry, otherwise I rested! I sat up, and Jenny threw her arms round me and said, 'Oh Mummy, I've known you *all* my life, haven't I, except for the first six weeks when I was with that horrible person who didn't want me?'

I said, 'But Jenny, it wasn't like that at all,' and I told her about her mother, who was fourteen, and who had sent a message for Jenny when we adopted her asking us to tell her that she loved her very much, but she was letting us be her Mummy and Daddy because she couldn't look after her properly. Both the children then asked many questions about their mothers and I told them what I knew, emphasising their care and concern. Michael's mother had made him a shawl, and so on. They asked if they could see their mothers and we talked about this hard point. They accepted it when I said I didn't know where they were and that perhaps it was better that way. (This will no doubt arise in their minds again.)

Michael, as usual, was matter-of-fact about everything, but Jenny was very much moved. So was I. I thought she would have a sleepless night. In fact, it was obvious that, with real compassion, she was thinking for me more than about herself. I remember saying to her, when she was shaking at bedtime, that there would be a sad little place in her heart, I knew, but most people do have sad places in their hearts and we were very, very lucky to have each other as parents and children, brother and sister.

The next day it was as though Jenny had lost a great burden. She has been like that ever since. She started a new school the following day, and it was as though she had moved on to a fresh course. She took to it like a duck to water. Our children are secure and confident, without being precocious or cheeky. I think this has probably developed from honesty in us and facing up to our needs as a family.

3   Parents and teenagers

MOST PARENTS WILL AGREE *that we go through the toughest times when our children become teenagers. Suddenly from being happy and outgoing, they become grumpy, rude, moody, self-centred and totally absorbed by their own circle of friends. Whatever the parents say seems to have no effect whatsoever. The need to be liked and approved of by their peers takes an almost unbreakable hold.*

What can we do? First, it might be helpful to take a look at ourselves. Do we as parents stand up for what we think and believe or do we bend too easily to the opinion of our peers? Do we pay too much attention to what our neighbours say or our friends at the club? Do we put pressure on our kids to be popular and push them into boy-girl relationships long before they are ready? Do we expect them to have the guts to say 'no' to drugs and drink while we think it is perfectly all right to smoke and drink ourselves?

And what about sex? Do we expect them to go along with the crowd or do we battle for them to accept Christ's standards of purity before marriage and faithfulness in marriage?

It is not what we say but how we live. There is a price to pay. We can't fool our children. They read us like a book. A few years ago Digna said to me, 'Every time you make fun of Daddy not being able to speak Dutch I think you do it to make him feel small and I have hated you for it.'

I believe faith is caught not taught. You can't give the measles to any one else unless you have got them yourself.

I always remember a friend asking us when our girls were quite small, 'What is your aim for your children?' We had never really thought about it, except that we wanted them to be happy and healthy and have a good education, the things everyone wants for their children.

But we realized there was more to her question and decided to ask God what should be our aims for our children. We got two very clear thoughts: 'You are meant to teach them to care for others as much as they care for themselves; and they are meant to find a faith that is like a rock inside them which nothing or nobody can take away.'

We agreed these were marvellous aims but felt totally helpless as to how to achieve them. Then it dawned on us that the only way we could possibly achieve them was by trying to practise them ourselves every day, regardless of how many mistakes we would make in the process.

Today our girls are in their twenties and I am grateful to say that both have a genuine faith which each found in her own way.

Digna left school at sixteen to train as a hairdresser. It was the only thing she wanted to do. Late one Saturday night, as I was lying awake, worrying and waiting for her to come home, it was as if God said to me, 'Trust me with Digna. She is my child. I love her even more than you do. If you worry it means you don't trust me. Leave her to me. She is growing up and trying to find her independence from you, that is a normal and healthy process.'

Many, many times Paul and I have had to choose trust instead of fear. Just a few months ago she had a very real experience of Jesus coming into her heart. It happened during a service of healing at a friend's church.

It was a miracle. She is like her old self again, outgoing and full of life and fun. It is as if God has given her back to us after some pretty difficult years.

What can a mother do if, coming home after midnight from a tiring nursing shift, she finds that her sixteen-year-old daughter has not yet returned from a party? This is how a Dutch friend met the situation:

I decided to go to bed and read while waiting for her. But I found myself getting more and more angry and was soon mentally rehearsing a long sermon with which to receive her. Then, very clearly, I knew this was the moment to ask God to give me the wisdom I needed. Unexpectedly I got the idea to start doing some of the things I was planning to do the next morning. I started cleaning the living-room.

Just as I was putting away the vacuum cleaner, Julie came in. It was two-fifteen in the morning. I was able to greet her with, 'You must've had a very good evening. I've just finished cleaning the room.' I saw her face change. She had obviously expected an angry tirade and had prepared herself for it. Now she lowered her defences and said she was sorry for being so late. She had not wanted to come home alone on her bicycle on a dark road, and had waited for her friends. She told me all about the evening—who was there, what they did—things she would never have told me otherwise. But she understood how worried I had been and that she could have telephoned to say she was going to be late.

When there is tension between us, it is not a question either of giving in for the sake of peace or of showing my authority with angry words and deeds. The need is to trust in God's wisdom and plan—that He will show me the right way if I really want to know.

An alternative to worrying about teenagers is illustrated by a friend from the United States.

One night my younger daughter, Mary, returned from a date. We were in bed but not asleep. I called to her, 'Glad you are home.' She came in, sat at the foot of our bed and said, 'Mother and Dad, Ann and I have been talking things over. You are so worried about us that all we feel is your concern. What we want to feel is your love.'

Her honesty did something to melt the coldness in my heart towards her and Ann, which had grown since they had been going around with a group at high school whom we did not care for.

Our next move was to get to know their friends, have them in our home, and invite them to go with us to our cabin on the river. By showing more love than concern we helped the children through those difficult teen years.

One morning at breakfast with the children I decided to get honest with them about the kind of person I had been. Having posed as a self-righteous mother, it was very hard for me to tell them about my cheating in school, taking things, and my relationships with boys and how I had a part in making the world they had to grow up in. I burst into tears, feeling they could never respect or love me again.

Then Ann said, 'Mother, I don't know why, but I've never loved you as much as I do right now. I want you to know I have lots of things to put straight, and I am going to start on them right away.'

One night, not so long ago we had a group of young people from various countries in our home. After we had all enjoyed our chilli con carne we sat around, talking. I had been asked by a local group of women to come and talk about teenagers the following Tuesday. I asked our young guests what had meant most to them in their own homes during their teenage years. These are some of their replies:

A Dutch girl: Doing things together as a family, going for walks, cycling, having family meals so you could tell about school.

A Norwegian girl: Rules are part of love, also discipline. Parents should try to make kids more dependent on God rather than on parents.

A German: Parents should trust their children more and help them find the real source of life. We live in a fatherless society—I have never had a real relationship with my father. We were always superficial; my father was never honest with me. So it is difficult for me to find a real relationship with my heavenly Father.

A South African girl: Parents should always be there and available to listen without condemning. Mothers should love their job as mothers.

A Canadian: My parents were divorced. I never knew what hopes they had for us kids. I really miss that.

A Chinese girl: My parents were so poor and had to work

so hard there seemed to be no time to do things as a family.

An American girl: My mother preached to me but her own life was a mess.

A Swedish girl: I am grateful my parents always treated me as a responsible person. They also shared their difficulties with me. Listening is caring.

An English girl: My parents showed me you don't need money to have a good time—we always made music together. They also taught me about forgiveness.

A Canadian girl: As parents don't let your kids talk you out of your values. My parents almost lost theirs because of my arguments.

A German: Parents should not push their children and not be too ambitious for them. When God is the father in the family a lot of strain is taken from the father.

A Swiss girl: Need to share difficulties in the family. It was hard for me to see my father cry but we could pray together.

An American girl: My parents believed in me even though I was going astray. They always told the truth about themselves and about me. Their objective with me was that I should have a relationship with God no matter what my relationship with them was like.

Here is the experience of another Dutch friend of mine, a busy woman with a large family:

My husband and I were very fortunate to have learned to listen to God when our eldest daughter was only four. As a matter of fact, she understood before us that praying also meant listening.

One day she said to us, 'You know, I can pray already.' When we asked, 'What do you say to God?' she replied, 'I don't say anything to Him—He says something to me.'

All through the many years of bringing up a family of seven we have been learning to listen together with the children, but also learning about it from the children.

Between the ages of four and fourteen listening to God had been normal practice for our daughter Helen, who had told her classmates about it. Then at fourteen she gradually stopped.

One day when she was fifteen my husband and I realised that she was going to ask us permission for something she wanted to do very badly but to which we could not agree. I foresaw a horrible clash of wills, tears and tantrums. To fortify ourselves we went down on our knees and promised God that we would not say yes to our children—if we felt He wanted us to say no.

The next morning Helen and I had breakfast together and after a few minutes she put her question to me. I said, 'Helen, Daddy and I went on our knees yesterday and promised God that we would never say yes if we felt He said no. The answer is no.'

There was complete silence. When she had finished eating she said goodbye in a friendly way and left. She didn't raise the subject again.

I stayed behind, grateful for the discovery I had made that when our children know their parents are sincerely trying to obey God, they do not want to get between God and us. So our obedience can help them accept His will, even if it sometimes goes against their own desires.

I have a German friend whose family owned large estates in what is now East Germany. They suffered great hardships during World War II, losing many relatives and all their possessions. She writes of what she went through as a teenager:

I thought it was absolutely unfair to be put into this world by two people whom I had to accept as parents. I hated life—

it held nothing but difficulties for me. As I grew older I learned to act sensibly, but the desperation and hopelessness never left me. I knew there was a living God, but how could He solve my problem?

One day I realised it was my love of desperation and hopelessness which divided me from the love of God, but I would not accept the implications of this discovery. So one dark night I took three times as many sleeping pills as a human being can bear.

I was found in time. For three days I was unable to see or speak, but I knew with perfect clarity that I had to make a decision. Finally I said, 'All right, God, you win,' and, more frightened than happy, I started a new life under new conditions.

I stumbled my way forward, step by step, and experienced the difference. When I ran into trouble and despair came up again, something inside told me not to stop there but to go forward. It no longer made sense to blame my parents, my teachers or circumstances; I had to find out where *I* was wrong. This new-found objectivity helped me to get a grip on life. And after some time I even realised that I had been called to life—specifically and definitely—to take responsibility, and as a result happiness came to me.

Here a young man of nineteen, whose parents were divorced when he was about eleven, writes to his father:

Dear Dad,

I never could accept the fact that I had to choose between you and Mom. I have hated you and I am sorry. I apologise also for my behaviour at home and for my selfishness. I have not been honest. My girlfriend spent a few nights at the house but as we had no relationship, you and I, I felt I could not tell you.

I am starting to find a faith. I believe God is the answer. My hatred for my home made me hate my country. Many problems came up because of my state of rebellion and not accepting help from you or anyone. I have not been as ungrateful as it may seem. If I can choose love for hate every thing will be well. It will be tough. I am frightened of doing things wrong.

I hope you are better and that this letter shows you my feelings and apologies.

Your son, Andrew.

I, too, in my teens was causing my mother sleepless nights. This was not so much due to any deep rift in the family as to all the things which she feared might fill the vacuum of purpose in my life.

I was born and brought up, along with my six brothers and sisters, in the lovely southern part of Holland called Brabant.

We had a happy childhood, in spite of coming face to face at an early age with bombings, shortage of food and concentration camps. Each of my parents had been imprisoned by the Germans before I was ten, but they had an unshakable faith that God was in control of our lives and not the Germans.

Several things stand out in my mind about these days: the Saturday nights when we played games as a family; my mother always waiting for us with a cup of tea when we came home from school, ready to listen to our stories; the time spent together on Sunday mornings when Dad would read a story from the Bible and Mum play hymns on our little organ. Our friends and cousins used to come to those mornings, too, and afterwards we would all play football, or Monopoly if it was raining.

My maternal grandmother had a big influence on my life. She had lost two sons when they were still in their twenties, but she was never bitter. She had a childlike faith and a tremendous 'joie de vivre'. She taught me to waltz when I was nine, and also my first words of English. After the war she would take me to see films and plays which my mother thought highly unsuitable. She also loved to play roulette and often won, though she always knew when to stop.

After finishing high school, where my reports generally

read, 'She could do better if only she would try'—there just seemed too little incentive to make me try harder—I went to live in Amsterdam. A girlfriend and I rented an attic in a three-hundred-year-old house on a canal where our beds shook every time a ship came by. We took jobs in a fashionable store where we learned how to make hats—as well as some of the facts of life which had escaped us before.

The next year I went to Paris to learn more French and more about fashion. My mother was worried about me, and she had reason to be. We were polite to each other, but I never told her what was going on inside me. She asked me that summer to go with her to Caux, a beautiful spot high above the Lake of Geneva, where Moral Re-Armament* had been holding conferences since 1946. There I met people of many classes and races, including young people who seemed to have a purpose in life, and a Hollywood actress to whom I felt I could talk.

After a few days it became clear to me that I must make a choice: either to go on as I was, totally centred on my own career and fulfilment, or to use my life for a bigger purpose. I began to realise that the world might be in this mess because of millions of self-centred individuals like me who never thought beyond what we wanted out of life.

One night I saw a play about life in a university. The first act shows life as it is today, free and easy. The second act shows the same university, but under a totalitarian regime, where people are controlled by fear and terror. As I was watching that second act it was as though my childhood in occupied Holland flashed in front of my eyes, and a voice inside me said, 'Do you want your children to go through that? If things go wrong in the world you won't be able to blame anyone else—you are too selfish to do anything about it.'

The next morning I felt utterly miserable. I knew that going back to enjoy the old life in Paris would no longer satisfy

---

* Moral Re-Armament, initiated by Dr Frank N D Buchman who came from Allentown, Pennsylvania, is a philosophy of life based on the experience that when a person listens, God speaks; when a person obeys, God acts; when people change, nations change.

me, but to decide to put my life into the hands of a higher authority, as my Hollywood friend suggested, was a very daunting prospect.

I went to find her. We talked for a long time, and finally we knelt down together and I said to God, 'OK, God, I give you my life, whatever it may mean.' It was like signing a contract, and I intend to honour it for the rest of my life. It was as if I had come out of a long dark tunnel into the bright light. There were many things I had to put right, especially with my mother. We became very good friends, which we still are today. That decision was the beginning of a way of life so adventurous and satisfying that I can recommend it to anyone.

How can parents prepare a teenager for life at university? Here is an English couple's story:

Our daughter got a scholarship to university. We were all very pleased and proud. She had nine months before starting there, and after years of hard schooling had a dizzying sense of being free to do innumerable things—a typing course, learning to drive, a trip abroad, etc. This was discussed endlessly. She was free to do what she wanted, within reason, but after a lifetime of taking decisions together in a time of seeking God's guidance, she valued the sense of security this brought and asked if she could decide her plans with us in this way.

However, we were getting tired of the whole subject and felt she only wanted us to agree to her plans, not really to find out what God wanted done in those nine months.

That morning my husband said to me, 'The world does not need one more self-centred intellectual. If she can only think about herself and her own plans, it would be better if she didn't go to university, but did something which would be of more use to other people.' I agreed, but the thought of telling her this was painful. Would we lose her trust and confidence for ever by being so blunt?

The moment of our confab arrived, and she came in rather self-importantly. Her father told her his thought straight away. Stunned silence. Tears began to flow, and then suddenly she said, 'I've just remembered I promised to meet so-and-so in ten minutes and I must go now.' She rushed out of the room and we looked at each other.

She came back later, her old cheerful self, and told her father he was absolutely right. A marvellous three weeks in Italy was followed by going to a summer camp where a new musical was being produced. She had done some producing and rather hoped to have a hand in it there, but when she arrived she found there was no one to cook. So she spent the summer—a rather wet one—living in a tent and cooking for a large number of hungry people, and felt it was a first-rate preparation for the academic life.

A Canadian mother writes:

Ross, who is thirteen, would hardly eat anything. He was weighing each calorie meticulously. Due to peer influences and pressures at school he was on the verge of becoming anorexic. As the pounds dropped off daily, my fears turned to panic.

In talking to other parents I began to see that you cannot be run by fear and faith at the same time. I also saw that Ross was using my fear to control me, to cause me sleepless nights and to become the centre of my attention.

So I decided to give over all my fear to God; to do this each day, and to live beyond personal concerns into the lives of others. Our children belong to God. How quickly He works. Three days later, Ross started to eat normally again and to live for something else besides his self image, his music for instance. In the following weeks, full health, strength and vitality were regained, plus a happy outgoing personality.

After my decision I felt totally free of fear or anxiety about Ross's health. I believe that parents, by protecting their children from hurts or by fighting their battles for them are ruining their character, making it harder for them to know how to live in the real world. Because their frustration tolerance was not properly developed we are now having to deal with masses of adults with teenage emotions and instability.

An American mother and father tell the story of their daughter's heartbreaking slide into drugs and her eventual rehabilitation.

My husband and I and our four children had a happy family life. But one day we had a very heavy blow—our youngest daughter, Cindy, died of a brain tumour at nineteen.

Susan, the second youngest, was already married and studying in California. When her sister was dying she came straight home. They had been very close and Cindy's sudden death affected Susan deeply.

She asked me one day, 'Mother, why do people have to suffer?'

'I can't tell you. All I can do is turn to God,' I replied.

45

My words gave her no comfort, for Susan had no faith.

Back in California she went into a heavy depression and began to smoke hashish. Later she took LSD. For her it was like a revelation. She felt as though she could understand life and death much better. She gradually became addicted, stopped her studies and moved from one hippy commune to another. Her marriage broke up.

I knew she took drugs. I was so desperate that I asked the help of the police in trying to find her. But there were so many young people reported missing that it was no good.

One day, out of the blue, Susan rang us from San Francisco. She gave us her address and rang off. I took the next train 3,000 kilometres right across America. I found her in an old shed in a slum district. The place was empty but for a dirty mattress.

Young people came in and stared at me. I knew I could accomplish nothing with words. It broke my heart to see those children. When I saw my daughter taking drugs I broke down in tears. I couldn't bear it.

She shouted at me, 'How dare you tell me what to do?' I had not said a word.

Next morning I rang my husband and asked him to come. He took the next plane, although he could ill afford the fare. When he arrived he looked around the shed and said, 'Susan, I am not staying in this hole a moment longer. If you want to talk to us, you must come with us.' His brother had lent us his weekend home in a nearby town, and to my surprise Susan agreed to come with us.

That night I had the feeling God wanted to shake me: 'You allowed yourself to be run by fear and not by faith. The stark fear of having to lose Susan as well as Cindy got hold of you. Susan will have to decide for herself how she is going to live. You must let go.'

The following morning I did feel free. I sensed an inner authority which was not my own. I said to Susan, 'We will never try to find you again. You must decide whether you want to go on living like this or to make a new start.'

She broke down and wept. In the days that followed we

were finally able to talk to each other in peace. She began to find herself again.

When she left she hugged us and said, 'I am so glad you came.' I was free of fear, although I knew she had not yet overcome the crisis and was in danger of committing suicide. But after that visit she phoned us once a week. Those conversations became a vital link. I told her what we were doing at home and that we loved her. I decided to believe that a miracle could happen.

Easter came. My husband and I sent Susan a beautiful Easter lily—we had always had one at home at Easter. Susan replied by return of post, 'You don't need to worry about me any more. I have finished with hippy life and with drugs too. It is as though I have been through the valley of the shadow of death and have come back to life. Thank you for believing in me just when nobody else did, not even me.'

She took up her studies again. The fears that her memory might have been damaged because of drugs were fortunately unfounded, and she got her degree.

All this has opened my heart to these young people, whatever they look like and however they are dressed. It used to be my child who looked like that. The most important thing we learned from this experience was never to judge. We could help others most of all when we were honest about our own needs.

I tried to get in touch with the parents of those other young people. I rented a room and put an announcement in the paper inviting people to a meeting. The first time ten came, the next week thirty-five. These parents, desperate about what had happened in their families, were looking for someone to talk to. At first some of them could not see what they could have done to help their son or daughter. But soon some began to break old habits like alcohol and smoking. And the new freedom they found gave them hope for their children too.

The work grew so much that we could not cope with it on our own. Eventually the Department of Health took it over. That was the beginning of the Anonymous Association of Parents of Drug Addicts.

A sure way to lose the respect of young people is to demand no standards of any kind. A young girl came to visit her boy friend in university, and was planning to sleep on the floor of his room. When a neighbouring family who knew her invited her to stay instead, her face lit up.

'That is marvellous,' she said. 'I could not understand why my father didn't object when I told him I was going to stay with Jack. I thought he must have stopped loving me or something.'

An Australian businessman tells what happened when his eldest son ran away from home.

Jim is the eldest of eight—five sons and three daughters. We were eleven around the kitchen table after adopting a young lad who became one of the family, sharing all our ups and downs. We were always close as a family and had great times together.

But one day—bang! Our son was off. We had had our bust-ups as well as our fun. Sometimes there were noisy threats to leave home as tempers flared. There were temporary walk-outs, but the thought of mother's cooking would always lure them back home. This was the first time one of them had walked out and not returned.

For my wife life had become quite difficult, as she tried to cope with my philosophy of, 'You run the home and look after the children. I've got enough to do running my business.' The idea may have been all right in theory, but because of my neglect of the family as a confirmed 'workaholic', I had forfeited their respect and credibility as a caring father.

As they got older my strong-arm methods of imposing my will just did not get them to 'see sense' as I thought they should. My wife, trying to be both mother and father, was getting worn out. Our blow-ups became more frequent as she tried to shield the children from my wrath when they refused to come to heel.

Then a new factor came in. Our youngest daughter came home from primary school and told us that her teacher had spoken to the class about 'listening for God's guidance.' Our daughter had sat quietly listening, and got the idea to tell us about keeping the money she had been given for Sunday school. She apologised. Then she had another thought—to double the amount out of her own pocket money and give it to the church.

She told us the teacher had suggested that you could find the right thing to do by taking the four standards of absolute honesty, purity, unselfishness and love, as guideposts to discover where you fall short. Then God's thoughts were more likely to get through.

Naturally my wife and I were pleased. I thought this was good for my daughter, and could help the rest of the family. They were thinking it would be good for me!

At this time the teacher was staging a play, *The Ladder* by Peter Howard, near our home. My wife and daughter went, and I accompanied them rather reluctantly. The play was about a man climbing to the top of the success ladder—prepared to sell his country's secrets to the powerful money-backers who had put him at the top. The more involved he got, the less he thought of his wife and home. The play climaxed with him making a clean break with corruption and with the speculators who were blackmailing him.

I was shaken by its reality. Afterwards I found myself talking with one of the actors. 'That was a powerful play,' I said to him. 'I am concerned what kind of society lies ahead for my children. I wonder what they will do about it.'

He looked at me intently and asked, 'Are *you* concerned? I wonder what *you* will do about it?'

Taken aback, I replied, 'That was a bit below the belt, wasn't it?' Right then and there I knew he was right. It was up to me to take a hand in making society the kind of place fit for families to grow up in.

Things began to come together for me; what my daughter had been telling us about 'listening', how the man in the play had faced up to himself and changed, and then this question put to me after the play. I thought of my son, estranged in another city; what was I meant to do?

I asked God to tell me what to do about Jim. My first thought was, 'Go and find him.' So we set out. We knew the name of the pop group he was playing with, and after some enquiries found where he was staying. We sat together in my car. Then I had to implement my second thought, which was to tell him that I love him. I found that difficult—how can you tell a man of twenty-five that you love him? But I did it.

I told him I had been wrong in my stubbornly-held attitudes, and that I felt these had contributed to the break in our relationship and getting him into the drug scene. I apologised. I told him of the help I had found in looking at myself and the situation in the light of those absolute standards.

He looked at me and said, 'Dad, there is one more absolute—absolute forgiveness.'

He came with us to lunch to meet some of our friends at the conference which we were attending at that time. He was always a keen cricketer, and was amazed to meet one of his favourites, Conrad Hunte, former Vice-Captain of the West Indies Cricket Team. What a lunch we had! It was the modern equivalent of the fatted calf reunion.

Some months later he was off drugs completely. My youngest son, who was on alcohol, mushrooms and other kicks, became free through the change and care of his older brother.

Here are parts of the letter Jim wrote us after we returned home:

I only discovered today what the true meaning of life is. Sure, in the past I knew that absolute truth and honesty was the true meaning of life, but I'd never done anything about it. Never done anything about all the untruths and greed I'd collected inside me. That is why I could not understand your wanting to apologise to me for past injustices—and no one can understand that until they are free themselves. And today I was freed—I prayed and suddenly I knew what had to be done. I'd known it all along, but I couldn't accept it. I find myself wanting to tell you all how badly I've treated you—how I stole money from Dad when you were a newsagent and later when I worked with you in the business—I'm truly sorry. And Mum, how I stole money from your purse, even in the bad times when there was very little in it. Again I'm truly sorry. . . .

I know now that the only way to repay all these things is to admit them and then do everything in my power to lead an honest and selfless life.

I will be home soon, your birthday, Mum, so see you then.   Love, Jim

'My work was so hard that I felt I could do nothing for the children. I had decided to quit teaching,' said Marisa. She teaches English to thirteen- and fourteen-year-olds in a government junior high school in Rio de Janeiro, Brazil.

There are forty students in each class. It is very difficult to teach a language to so many. They come from under-privileged homes and see no point in learning English. Most of them will have no opportunity to use it. Also I don't have any equipment such as tape recorders to use with them.

My aunt gave me a copy of the Portuguese edition of *Listen to the children* and I read it when I went on holiday. It made me think. I realized that I talked a lot but never listened. I was always complaining that my students were difficult and that the school was not as I would like it. I was always protesting in teacher's meetings. Yet I did not listen to others, let alone God.

I also thought that I would like to pass on to my students the ideas contained in the book. Instead of just passing on knowledge, I wanted to help them become better human beings.

I decided to spend fifteen minutes at the beginning of each lesson discussing the ideas contained in certain words such as honesty, love, unselfishness, respect, responsibility, purity, forgiveness, obedience and, lastly, liberty, which is the result of all the others.

At the first class of the year, I arranged the students in a circle and asked them to write their answers to questions such as 'Who am I? What sort of student was I last year? What am I going to do this year? How can I become a better person? Is it important to come to school on time? Why?' I wanted them to think and answer the questions honestly.

Then I put their answers in an envelope and sealed it and told them I wouldn't open it. I did not want them just to write things to please me.

At the end of that lesson I did something which I had never done before. I asked them to pray in silence for the coming year and what they would like it to be. As they have different creeds I asked them to do it in silence.

For the rest of the term I took each of the words in turn. I wrote thought-provoking questions on the board and the students wrote down their thoughts. Some volunteers were ready to read to the class what they had written. Then the English lesson would be resumed.

After this time of reflection the students were much more peaceful. The discipline in the class was better. They still found English difficult, but they were more interested. Those first fifteen minutes were easily made up because we worked so much better afterwards.

I had intended to do this only for the first term, but at the request of the students they continued throughout the year. At the end I went back to the questions I had asked the first day, asking the students to reconsider them. Then I gave them back those papers which I had sealed in the envelope. They were amazed to see how their ideas had changed. They felt they had grown up.

On one occasion when we were talking about honesty, one of the pupils asked if I had ever cheated in exams. I had to admit that I had on several occasions. I learned that it was more effective to pass on moral values by showing myself to be an ordinary human being, than just by making speeches.

We teachers tend to believe we have the answer to everything. I used to underestimate my pupils. I found they could give excellent definitions of abstract words. One told me, 'Love is a deep friendship which can change the world and put an end to wars.' Another said, 'To be honest means not to take advantage of other people.'

To transmit knowledge is important. The students will need this during their lives. Yet it is more important to know ourselves as we really are, to know where we are going in life and to have hope and faith.

4   Educating parents

ONE OF OUR *Canadian friends was the late Dr Gustav Morf, the Montreal psychiatrist who interviewed most of the political prisoners who were responsible for terrorising Quebec in the sixties. His book,* Terror in Quebec, *has become a minor classic, as similar groups have appeared all over the world.*

Talking to the Quebec terrorists, Dr Morf immediately saw that they were not the children of economically poor homes, but rather 'the offspring of an affluent, self-indulgent and permissive society'. 'They know what they want and they want it quick, or else,' he wrote. 'They are blackmailing a society where blackmail in marriage, in industrial relations and in politics has become commonplace and where almost everyone demands much more out of life than they are prepared to give.'

Dr Morf noted that the common symptom was 'immaturity'. 'The most dangerous person,' he stated, 'is the one who keeps the immaturity, the outlook, the rebellion and the relative responsibility of an adolescent, while exercising the full powers of an adult.' But why did this immaturity persist?

'The small child today,' Dr Morf concluded, 'has more difficulty in adjusting to reality than in the past. Too many remain maladjusted throughout their childhood,' while still more 'refuse, in adolescence, to grow up,' so that they remain 'eternal adolescents' or 'eternal students'. This is probably due, in most cases, to 'the over-stimulation provided by modern life and to the moral confusion and permissiveness of parents'. Their children 'no longer know the difference between right and wrong'.

Dr Morf's insights throw a heavy responsibility upon us parents. Our own experience is that many young people in fact want to take a mature attitude to the world, that they would like to invest their lives in a society which works and which would enable the needs of the entire human family to be met. They are aware that this is the first century in which it is technically possible to feed, house and clothe all mankind, and they are frustrated by the failure of our generation to tackle the problem adequately. They react against our love of comfort and material preoccupations—and the reactions which we condemn in them are often protests against our high talking and low living. 'Older people drink and get high and feel great,' wrote the underground paper International Times. 'And we do other things and get high and they spit on us.'

So mature parents are as necessary as mature adolescents. As one seventeen-year-old girl said to me recently, 'I have learnt that every decision I make affects other people. There are no private decisions.'

Honesty can set up a chain reaction. A Swiss friend writes:

A few months ago I stood in one of the romantic little streets of Old Lucerne feeling deeply ashamed of myself. I had just lied to an unsuspecting sales assistant at the chemist's in order to obtain a particular medicine available only on prescription.

When she had asked me if a doctor had prescribed the medicine I replied, 'Yes,' with great conviction. I was shocked at myself. Not that I wanted to misuse the medicine in any way, but I had just lied to get what I thought I needed.

I thought of our eight-year-old daughter Gretel who is constantly bombarded with confusing and unhelpful influences at school, in the neighbourhood and on television. My husband and I are concerned to give her the freedom and firmness of character which come from not needing to whitewash anything and always being able to listen to the quiet voice of your conscience.

At lunch I told our daughter what I had done. She looked at me intently and suggested I take the medicine back. I replied, 'I don't think chemists can take back goods they have already sold, but perhaps I should go back and tell them I lied to them.'

The afternoon went by as usual with school, chores and homework. In the evening Gretel was particularly restless and aggressive. After supper is the time when we pray and sing with her, and we often talk about the things which are most on our minds. That particular evening everything seemed to go wrong. Gretel got more and more impudent, and I felt both helpless and a failure as a parent. With a curt, 'All right then, we won't pray. Sleep well,' I left the bedroom.

I sat in the sitting room feeling depressed and uneasy. Suddenly two little arms slid round my neck and a voice sobbed, 'I don't want to be like that. Sometimes a little devil gets into my heart when I don't want it to.' Between the sobs some of the things tumbled out which had been going on in her heart in the last weeks.

We talked about it all quietly, and then prayed for the various difficulties. 'Now she will sleep in peace,' I thought, and went to bed.

There came a knock on our bedroom door. The child was standing there in her nightdress. 'I must tell you something else I never told you before. A few weeks ago I thought I would rather have our neighbour as a mother because she is kinder. I am so sorry, because I *do* love you most of all.'

Back to bed—peace again—and then another knock. 'Mummy, when Daddy and I dropped that tray full of crockery a year ago I always said it was Daddy's fault, but it was mine. I want to give you all my pocket money to pay for the broken china.' Her face was radiant as she added, 'There, now we really have made peace!'

Next morning I went to the chemist. Standing at the door, I felt very stupid. Three sales assistants enquired if they could help. I wasn't sure if any of them was the one who had served me the previous day, but I simply said that I had lied to obtain some medicine. That started a lively and very friendly discussion with the employees.

When I got home Gretel wanted to know exactly what had happened.

This experience is like an anchor in her life, which holds fast despite storms and currents. With a character like mine—and my daughter has a good dose of it—things cannot but go wrong sometimes, but when they do Gretel looks at me and says, 'Remember when we made peace?'

A Canadian teacher told me this story of how an Indian mother helped her son to get over his stuttering;

Farham was a sixteen-year-old boy who very much wanted to become a doctor, but thought it would be impossible because of his bad stutter. When I was in bed in India with blood poisoning, his mother Mani used to come and visit me. She often mentioned Farham's disability, and one day I asked if he had always stuttered. She replied that he had not stuttered until he was five years old. I asked her why he had suddenly begun to stutter. She said she didn't know, but I was sure she did.

One day I suggested that we listen to the inner voice and ask God how Farham could be helped. For some days she had no thoughts. Then she decided to be honest with me. She had been angry with Farham over some small thing when he was five and shut him outdoors after dark for two hours. Farham had been terrified and from then on he had stuttered.

I suggested Mani be honest with Farham. This she did not want to do because she feared what Farham would think of her, but after another time of quiet she decided to do it.

The result was as she expected. Farham turned on her and asked, 'How could you do this to me?' Mani believed she had done the wrong thing.

A few days later, again listening together, Mani hit on the idea of having a nice snack ready for Farham when he came back from school. Farham ate the snacks, but was very distant with his mother and would have nothing to do with her.

This went on for some weeks, till one day Mani had the thought to knit Farham a pullover. When he came home from school he pointed to the pullover and asked, 'For me?' Mani nodded. Farham ran over to his mother, threw his arms around her and told her he loved her. From that moment he stopped stuttering.

Mani came running over to see me, tears streaming down her face, saying, 'Farham has stopped stuttering, he has stopped stuttering!'

A schoolteacher from Berlin discovered new qualities in his eleven-year-old son:

It was a rainy Sunday afternoon. I had been busy correcting papers and preparing lessons for the next day. I suddenly felt like relaxing and doing something different.

In the room next to my study my wife was doing some very important accounts which she had to submit to a board early in the week. My tentative efforts to get a conversation

going were politely but firmly rejected. No wonder, after each addition she got a different total. So I drooped off back to my study and sank into a chair. I started to feel very sorry for myself. All sorts of lamentations suddenly welled up out of my subconscious, formulating themselves into questions: what sense is there in working hard? what sense is there in life itself? Dark thoughts were gathering inside me like a storm.

At that moment, Lukas, our youngest, came home from a friend's house. His cheeks were red from running, his eyes brimful of life. I felt compelled to take him into my confidence and tell him my misery.

'I am in a bad way, Lukas. Can you help me?'

He looked at me in astonishment. Was Dad joking or was he really in trouble? He quickly pulled up a chair, sat himself in front of me and said, 'O.K. Out with it.'

I told him everything and it seemed as though it was not my young son but a friend, a soul mate who was listening to everything with great patience.

When I had finished he gave a deep sigh and suggested, 'Let's pray about it.' 'You start,' I said. And Lukas prayed, out loud, for me, for our family, and for the needs in the world, and while he was praying, slowly the sun came up again for me.

About the same time my wife finished her accounts, our second son came home and after a happy meal we had a good evening together playing games and reading stories.

A woman from a Muslim country sends these reflections:

'I'm stubborn. I never change my mind.'

'Don't argue. Do as I tell you.'

Such remarks get people's backs up. Under the calm surface one may feel anger, resentment, despair.

I began to understand this kind of conflict when I made the unexpected discovery that I was programmed with an Automatic No. I began to observe the operation of the Automatic No in myself and others. It seemed that no matter what came up—a new suggestion in our women's club, the desire of one of the children to go to a cinema—my first reaction was No. Later on I might take a more positive attitude.

It was not really a change of mind, since in the first place there was no reflection, just the triggering of a ready-made response. The reasoned response came later and might be Yes, No or Maybe.

My next discovery was that my husband had a similar automatic response which made him too say No. That explained a lot of the mutual irritation which we endured.

Then followed the need to tell my children, my husband and some colleagues that I had an Automatic No, and to warn them not to take my first reaction as final. 'Just give me a little time,' I told them.

At home when I had to make a decision I sometimes said, 'If you want my answer now, it is No, so you'd better come back in half an hour and see what I'll say.' This worked much better!

One day while my husband was out I was practising giving him a piece of my mind, stabbing the air with my finger to emphasise my point. Suddenly I remembered the 'secret weapon' a friend had given me. I looked at it—my hand, with one finger pointing accusingly at my husband and the three others pointing straight at me.

I asked myself, 'Although the things you say about your husband may be true, just what are you yourself that he should be devoted to you? Really you are lucky that he has put up with you for so many years. How do you show your love for him? You never miss a chance to needle him, especially in public. Why, you even use your own children to hurt him, because you know his weak points and can egg them on by saying, "Ask your father this, and ask your father that." '

I recognised that the time had come for me to change before it was too late. If I loved my husband, I had to start showing it.

Then one day came an experience we had never had before—my husband in prison, myself out of a job, one child at school, social life cut off. I was afraid that our small community—mother and son—might become neurotic. I asked God what I could do. The answer was simple and clear, 'Listen.'

I couldn't really see what good would come of listening, but I decided to try it. So when my son came home I resisted the temptation to take up time and pollute the atmosphere with all the things on my mind. Much to my surprise, he began to make comments and ask questions which showed his hopes and fears. For instance, he asked, 'If someone curses me in the bus, what should I do?'

This was years ago, but I shall never forget the broad avenues of experience and understanding which opened up when I began to listen.

It is not easy to find a common language in religion. The terms used by one person may be full of meaning and emotion for him, but may be empty words for the other. My husband is a Muslim and I am a Christian. Through listening to the inner voice we found that common language.

An American mother admits that her family did not turn out according to her dreams.

All my life the only thing I wanted was to be a mother. I even call myself a professional mother. Yet somehow my family didn't turn out the way I'd dreamed. For sure, when the children were babies I had good fun 'playing dolls' and then 'playing teacher', so much so that I didn't notice where I was falling short of my goal as the 'mother' who built up character.

Our eldest son was the first to challenge all my ingenuity and psychology. He arrived by Caesarean section, and thus began his individual approach to the whole of life, doing things his own way. Before he was a year old he could climb over the high side of his crib, and by a year and a half he was climbing the six-foot fence around the yard. At five he was building a boat in our basement. His teacher opened my eyes to the wonder I was overlooking when she commented, 'Isn't it wonderful to have such an enterprising young son!'

Three years later a church friend opened my eyes again when she asked the women present to pray for each member

60

of their families, thanking God for something special about each person. The tears streamed down my cheeks when I came in my prayer to this child. I could think of nothing positive to thank God for. I went home and began to look more closely for what was good and positive in him and to praise God for him. Actually, that was what he needed, because by this time there were two younger children and he was scarcely noticed unless he acted up. I recognised then that I had to notice him when he was good to save him the need to be bad!

Children know right from wrong. But they need to face their own consciences, from which there is no escape. This is what showed up my failure as a mother. Each of our children has fallen into temptations against which God could have strengthened them, or where the application of absolute standard would have seen them through safely—temptations to steal, to cheat, to play hookey, to deceive, to experiment with drugs and sex.

So how did my husband and I react when our children let us down? Early in the game we reacted in anger and hurt pride. But that didn't help bridge the communication gap. In fact, our eldest son asked me several times whether we wanted to drive him from home, as our neighbours did their son.

I've learned to say, 'When I get control of my feelings, we'll talk.' And then in the calmness we talk and we listen. And usually an idea comes which helps me either in handling my feelings or in knowing what to do next.

Our eldest son moved in with his girlfriend shortly after we went overseas. We were hurt by their decision and fearful of their suffering further hurt together. But in retrospect we realised that many of our feelings stemmed from our own hurt pride. If we could set that aside and keep communications open, perhaps we could help them and strengthen their relationship into the permanent loving one we wished for them.

So we wrote them about our feelings, disappointments, fears and hopes, and they replied with theirs. And when, in their own good time, they made plans for their wedding, our son wrote, 'Things are getting better all the time, and I think it's because of the wonderful support from you.' (Our only support to them had been our acceptance and love in spite of our first reactions.)

In many ways I consider myself a failure as a mother. Time will tell. But I would like to be one of the people who help other mothers—tomorrow's parents—approach the career of parenthood with a little more preparation and a lot more help than I had. It takes more than just devotion and love to make good parents.

Reading the following stories, sent by a Swedish journalist, I felt I could identify myself with many of the incidents she describes.

When I married I had a vision of how a true Christian family ought to be. It was a beautiful theory, which has not worked out at all in fact. But what I have found is that there is a road to go for every woman, whatever her husband thinks or believes. God can show the most marvellous ways of finding the very best in each one of the family and use it to create unity. The thing is, someone has to start, someone has to listen to Him. If there is a family with one listener, there is total and marvellous hope. I say this after nineteen years' experience.

When the children were small there was always a battle between television and going to bed. They were not allowed to see any programme after seven o'clock in the evening. Sometimes we had to lock the door to the TV room, and they banged on it, threw shoes or other things and screamed outside. It was terrible. I had to find a solution.

I sat down to listen. Immediately a question came to my mind, 'Have you given them all they need before going to bed? Have you read to them, prayed with them, kissed them goodnight, tucked them in?' My answer was, 'No.' There were TV programmes I wanted to see, and I left the children so as to see these programmes. Next question: 'Which is more important—your desire to watch TV or your calling as a mother to give the children the peace and care they need before going to sleep?'

My decision was to stop looking at TV before the children were in bed. Peace was restored to the house. When I had told the children about my selfishness and my decision, it happened sometimes that they generously said, 'Mum, why don't you go and watch the TV now? We'll go to sleep all right.' They were then two, four and eight.

Bedtime battles did not stop as the years passed, but rather increased. They never wanted to go to bed at the right time. What should I do? Let them sit down and think out what the right time for each one should be. Oh, my—why hadn't I thought of that before? When children are asked themselves to decide, they are so stern, so moral, and they love to obey their own orders. The youngest one, aged four, thought she should go to bed at six o'clock; the next one at seven, and the next at eight. No more battles! But every birthday the first thought was, 'Now I am one year older. I can go to bed half an hour later.' It still works for the two youngest, now eleven and thirteen years old!

Our youngest daughter is very sensitive. When she was five she started to blink nervously. It didn't appear to be a physical sickness. Gradually it disappeared, but other things followed, culminating when she was eight when her whole body began to shake. She was laughed at in school and we didn't know what it was until the school nurse suggested we go to a psychologist. So there we were. I took her each week for some months and then we, her parents, were called in. We had four sessions with the psychologist. They were terrible.

We discovered that our daughter could not take disunity between her parents. This was the real reason behind the symptoms.

She expressed it herself one day like this: 'Mum, it gives me great pain when Dad is hard on you, because I love you. But it hurts just as much when you hurt him, because I love him.' Our decision to try to be united and solve our disagreements without tempers flaring has helped to solve her problems.

One evening just after our second son was born I was very tired and under pressure. The evening meal needed to be prepared, night clothes laid out, etc. I got more and more irritated, and the atmosphere grew more and more tense. Then my four-year-old came up to me, put his hand on my arm and said with concern, 'Mum, go to bed. You know what'll happen otherwise!' What would happen? Should I accept such humiliating clarity from my little son? All my maternal prestige rose up in protest. He stood there, calm and confident, and said with a slight smile, 'I will take care of the little one.' I went to bed and peace returned to the home.

When the children grew older they started helping us parents to find unity when we were at odds; this was especially true of our daughter. One day my husband and I had had a row. She came to me in the kitchen and said, 'Mum, can't you forgive Daddy?'

To my shame, I had to admit that this time it was just one time too many. 'I am bitter, and I just can't.'

She leaned over the kitchen table and said very steadily and intently, 'But, Mum, you just say, "Forgive me." That's all. It's so simple. Just one word. Forgive. Well, I know it is difficult at first, but then when you have said it, it is very simple and wonderful.'

I sat there, my heart stone dead.

She asked, 'Couldn't you make some coffee?' We often drink what we call 'reconciliation coffee'. Slowly I went to the stove, still stiff and sour. She heard her father coming downstairs, and she looked at me, standing full of tension in the middle of the kitchen. He stopped in the doorway, looking hesitatingly at me. I said slowly (it was really difficult), 'Do you want some coffee?' This meant, 'Forgive me.'

He rushed to the stove, embraced me happily and said, 'Yes, thank you!' And there was our girl jumping up and down shouting, 'I did it, I did it! I said to Mum to do it!' And she took a ginger cookie, broke it in three pieces, and we silently ate a piece each, knowing all was well—thanks to her!

Another time we were quarrelling in the kitchen. Our daughter heard it and rushed to her room. After half an hour she came down. 'Is it all right now?' she asked. 'Are you friends?'

'Yes,' I said, 'we are friends.'

'I know,' she said proudly, 'I know you are because I prayed for you!'

My husband I are both hard-working people. I travel a lot and I always used to manage to do too much and then arrive home exhausted. During the first years of our marriage he was furious with me and tried to forbid my journeys. Then I found out that with his help I could organise them sensibly. I had been too independent, not knowing how much joy there is in sharing the plans and burdens!

All the same, one day my husband said 'No' to a special journey. I was furious, then sad. Finally I had a thought, 'Why not decide as a family?' I tried to arrange a family council. Impossible. You just have to take the inspired moment, such as sitting around the kitchen table in the sunset after a good dinner. I put the problem on the table. And the children openly said what I never thought they would dare to say.

'Dad, you are a dictator if you forbid Mum to go on this journey,' said the eleven-year-old.

To our surprise my husband quietly answered, 'Do you think so? Maybe I am.'

Our little nine-year-old daughter said, 'We can do without you, Mum, for ten days. We have Daddy.'

And my husband said, 'Why don't we take a family trip first together, and then we can see you off on the plane?' So it was decided and everybody was happy.

There are many more stories to tell, but these are the ones I remember just now. When I see the children the way they are today, and think back to the rather stormy childhood they had, and the maturity they now possess, I know for sure that it is a grace. When I see my husband and myself, married for nineteen years 'for better, for worse' through all the conflicts and sorrows, pains and joys, I know that too is a grace. Maybe faithfulness in listening to the inner voice has played a part in keeping faith alive. Without a living faith I don't know how you can keep a marriage going or have family unity.

The wife of a Japanese industrialist writes:

I used to think my husband needed to change his way of life somewhat, while I had no imperfections because I was always right. My husband felt the opposite! But then I began to see that I had been wrong and I did need to change.

One morning my husband told me very frankly and honestly about his mistakes and apologised to me. I was so thankful for his honesty—but a month later we had a difference of opinion again. I was irritated. One of my friends suggested I should write down everything I was thinking about my husband, so I began to write. I had bad feelings towards him. It was a great shock to me when I realised that I had not forgiven him even the small faults he had confessed.

Soon after I had a high fever and was confined to bed for a few days. During that time I felt very strange things. I felt Jesus was beside me and He was so friendly, trying to console me. I realised how badly I had treated my husband, how deeply I had injured other people's feelings, while thinking I was doing the right thing.

One day my daughter suddenly stopped going to school. I did not know how to help her. A friend wrote to me and said, 'My heart always beats for your family, and my affection for you and faith in you are not separated by time or distance. God will hold you fast hour by hour, day by day, if you let Him. That daughter of yours is a fine person. Battles in life are inevitable, but you will win them all with the peace of those who trust in God.'

It was quite a shock to read those words—'if you let Him'. Until that time I thought that I had to do everything myself, and that meant that I did not trust God. I was very afraid of committing myself to Him. Then I realised that the tender feeling I received from that letter was not from a human being, but from God. And this kind of love is everlasting. I decided to commit everything into the hands of God, whatever might happen. In the course of time my daughter returned to school. And she became a fine person, just as if a bud had suddenly burst into flower.

One day I read a story, *Prisoner of Mao* by Jean Pasqualini, and I received a great shock. I know so many people are suffering in Asia while we are enjoying our free life here in Japan. Thanks to our economic development we Japanese are not suffering from hunger as we did during the war, but we have lost some of our friendships. We have to do something for these other people of Asia. If we continue in our selfish way Japan will come to destruction.

When we were given our first grandson I thought, 'It is our

duty to build a better society by the time he grows up.' I would like to leave him light and hope to lead him in future. Who is going to take responsibility in Asia? Japan must be a lighthouse in Asia.

Much is being written about the reconstituted family and its complications. Therefore it is encouraging to read how a Scandinavian friend tackled her situation:

I had been living alone in my own flat for ten years, enjoying my studies and my job when, seven years ago, I married Peter, a widower. During the first year of our marriage my greatest desire was to be alone with him and to concentrate on the fantastic feeling of being married for the first time in my life. But it was not to be.

Peter already had two children—Bess, aged 12, and Ivan, 10. They were always there, as eager as I was to share in the newness of the situation. I soon found myself feeling that our marriage would have been happier without them.

Some days I would come home dead tired and just want to be alone or with Peter. I found it difficult to make room for the children in my heart and life. By the time I had tidied up the mess at home or got involved in whatever was on their minds, I had no time or energy left to do the things that I had planned to do that evening. Even when I followed the advice of some of my friends—that the children were old enough to take care of themselves and I should not bother with them—it never worked. You cannot ignore children when they are living in the same apartment!

Of course I had met the children before marrying their father. In fact, I felt that my relationship with each child was better before our wedding. They used to visit me in my nearby flat. However, the four of us hardly ever spent time together. After I moved in with them, it was difficult to find the new group dynamics, especially as the three of them had established an exceptionally strong bond between them.

Inwardly I blamed the children for the problems which cropped up in my relationship with Peter. In fact the only quarrels we have had have been about the children. All this made me very unhappy.

However, we began to find some solutions. I decided that I must talk things over with Peter and also with Bess and Ivan. This helped a great deal. I was often surprised to discover that the children's thinking was drastically different from what I expected; and that they were quite capable of discussing matters seriously and appreciating other points of view. I found it was helpful to admit my faults to them. They became more forgiving when I admitted that I was wrong to lose my temper, for example, and I found it easier not to do the same thing again.

One day I had been rather negative to Bess in the morning. She came home from school with a surprise gift for me which she had bought with her pocket money. I knew I did not deserve any gesture of love from her and that melted the ice I had in my heart towards her.

This can be a two-way process. Once, when I was wishing she did not exist, I asked her for a walk. By the time we returned home I knew that she was a sweet person, full of fears and hopes. She needed my care and love.

Reading *The Greatest Thing in the World* by Henry Drummond was a revelation. His description of the loveless soul fitted me perfectly. I realised that I was responsible for the problems in our family. I saw that I am called to love others even if they do not love me or are not 'worthy' of my love. I started to see that difficult relationships in the family can help us to grow. If there were no problems how could I practice love, patience and unselfishness?

I still found the children restricting at times. I did not like the fact that they took so many things for granted—having fashionable clothes, travelling abroad, and above all expecting me to fit into the unchanging role of 'parent' while they were constantly changing. But now I try to see the childrens' positive side and not just focus on their pushiness or wanting their own way. Most important of all, I believe, is to have faith in each child. Without that, how can you expect them to change for the better?

5 Family power

FOR HIS BOOK Divorced Kids Werner Troyer interviewed *many children and teenagers who came from broken homes. One of his conclusions was that divorce can have a more devastating effect on a child than the experience of surviving a concentration camp.*

My daughter recently got a letter from a friend aged thirteen who had run away from her father's home and had gone to live with her mother. 'Monday I moved over to Mum's home. Dad called me that night. The next day I went over to Dad's house to talk to him and he started to cry. I was crying too of course, but it was worse to see him cry. That must have been the saddest day of my life.'

A friend of mine who is a teacher had a very difficult boy in her class, who was always fighting with other boys. He was about fifteen. One day she asked him why he behaved the way he did. His reply was, 'You know, Miss, my Mum went to live with the man next door and when that happens to you you feel like smashing everything.'

A divorced and remarried friend wrote me recently, 'If we could realise earlier what a break-up and a new marriage involve and the misery they cause our children, wouldn't we work a great deal harder to make the first marriage work?'

Is the highest function of the home simply to perpetuate life—or to create a way of life worth perpetuating?

Marriage does not need to deteriorate into a drab routine from which we long to escape. It becomes dull when we lose sight of its purpose. The family is the ideal training ground to prepare children to go out into the world. In the family they learn to consider the needs of other people. If they see their parents working through their differences and not giving up when things get tough it helps them to form stable relationships themselves. I believe the family unit can become a source of power for transforming society.

An English mother of three children writes:

Listening together. This has been an interesting experiment. When my husband first said, 'Let's try it,' we sometimes got the same ideas and were thrilled because we really felt the same Spirit was speaking to both of us.

But one morning I got a picture in my mind of all the bottles of drink in the sideboard in our dining-room. I felt compelled to clean out that cupboard, and I could see it in my mind's eye, neat and tidy but with no room in it for the alcohol. I just couldn't face the idea of throwing out those bottles—think of all the money they had cost us!

I wrestled with this for weeks.

Meanwhile we both stopped getting thoughts from God. Something had blocked our communication. I did not dare tell my husband this thought I had had about the drink. When I finally did, he said he would help me each time I wanted to give in to the desire to stock up our drinks cupboard for guests and dinner parties. I was, and am, so grateful to him, because not only has my desire gone to serve stiff drinks all the time, but my own dependence on alcohol as a stimulant and a screen for nervousness has disappeared. Now we do not feel it necessary to serve drinks when we are entertaining and we have no more alcohol in the sideboard. Blair and I have grown closer through his being able to understand and help me with my problem.

After this step, the behaviour of the children, aged five and six, which had started to deteriorate when we were entertaining in this way, improved noticeably. I had been worried about two specific things in my eldest child—a developing whine during the day and coughing a great deal at night. I was sure that they were a result of something wrong in my life, and it was when I began to face and deal with the drink problem that these problems in her went away.

72

The important thing to me is not the alcohol, but the fact that if there is something in our lives that we haven't faced honestly with God, then it is bound to cause hang-ups of one sort or another which directly affect the family.

Recently there was a flare-up between my husband and me. I swallowed my pride and suggested we listen to God for help. Blair agreed we really needed it. At once I began thinking about our courtship. It came up before my eyes like a film—one event led to another. Then I had the uncomfortable realisation that I had deceived Blair from the very beginning of our relationship, pretending I was a 'footloose and fancy-free' type who didn't give a damn about marriage or family life or settling down or even whether he were here today and gone tomorrow. In fact, I cared desperately underneath and wanted him to ask me to marry him.

Then I had the even more uncomfortable realisation that the Lord was asking me to tell Blair all these things, without modifying any of it. Shortly before this time we had both made a new commitment to God, telling Him we meant to live our lives according to His will to the best of our ability. I knew that if I had meant what I said, then I had better go and tell Blair the truth, which is what I did.

Blair only said, 'You know, I am very relieved to hear that you are human like the rest of us. I think our relationship will be smoother and less complicated as a result of what you have told me.'

This has happened, and instead of feeling humiliated by this experience I feel freed.

A Swiss mother suggests that children can be courageous, and stand up against peer pressure.

We enjoy our family life. Our two daughters are only twelve and ten years old and we are entering the teenage stage. Our long-term objective has been to make them ready for a world which moves fast—that is, ready for change as well as faithful to permanent values. Both these qualities are rooted in a deep personal friendship with their Maker.

I had always worried about bad influences, and lying awake

one night, afraid of the flood of permissiveness, selfishness and dirt which the children had to face, a thought struck me: 'Do you accept that your children, even at their early age, can be courageous, standing up against the dictatorship of permissiveness, and suffering for it if necessary from comrades or teachers?'

Of course the thing I hate most in life is to see my children suffer. But what is the good of my praising courageous people who risk their security and their lives, and yet not wanting my children to pay the price of unpopularity? Lying there in the darkness I said 'Yes' to whatever would come, and my fear vanished.

The interesting thing was that, in the same period, our twelve-year-old took a clear stand among her schoolmates, who are all bigger and stronger than she is. She was laughed at when she said, for instance, that she did not want a boy friend at least until she was eighteen (a very grown-up age in her eyes) and if she had one it would be for marriage and nothing else. We had never given her advice on the subject, but she was very firm, refusing any compromise. For a few weeks she was the centre of nasty attacks and was often in tears, but this finally stopped and she was fully accepted and they started having a lot of fun in the class. Of course, we are not through—who ever is? We're only beginning adolescence. But I have seen to my amazement that these very young ones know right from wrong and can show remarkable courage.

I once asked the two children separately, 'What gives security to a child?' and the answer from each was instant—'The parents.' After a while the older one added hesitatingly, 'And God.'

From what he sees among colleagues and their children, my husband Michel feels an important element is children knowing for sure that their parents will not separate, whatever difficulties or differences may occur.

The second factor is the security of parents themselves. If parents find security (for us personally it lies in God), the children are more likely to have it too. The security the parents do or do not have, deep down in their hearts, makes all the difference.

In January last year my husband, an architect, had a big cut in his salary, and even the danger of unemployment. For a few days I had to battle with fear and depression. The children knew the facts and the older one especially was affected by it. At night I would worry about all the possibilities of being short of money and of being humiliated, and how my husband would suffer from it. Again, I had to say 'Yes' to the hardness of life, and leave it all to God; at once peace and trust came back to me and the whole family. The readiness of the children for sacrifice and economy was a joy too.

Another important element Michel feels is to give enough time to the children so that they can come out with their feelings and questions. He unstintingly gives his spare time to having fun or working with the children. Perhaps that partly explains why they do not yet feel the need for a boy friend.

Two very important people are the grandmothers (unfortunately both grandfathers had died before the children were born). One grandmother lives with us. This means sacrifice for all three generations, but we see the riches of it again and again. Grand'mami has time for the children and she has more perspective and peace. When you go into her room you can feel it. When she came to live with us she made the wise decision that the children were ours to bring up, not hers; she would not interfere, only give what she had to give. This she does, and the children will never forget their times with her. I understand why Krushchev felt that he could not root out faith in Russia because of the grandmothers.

On the other hand, children give to old people the things which we, the very busy ones, are not always ready to give. Seeing the weakness of old age, children can show compassion and care with all the freshness and joy which they bring.

Often people say to my mother, 'You are lucky to live with your children.' Others say to me, 'You are lucky to have your mother with you.' This is all very true, on certain conditions! First, we need to be drastically honest together about what we feel, otherwise bitterness creeps in and impatience or fear. When things are talked out, solutions come naturally and we often end up with a good laugh. Second, both sides must be open to change and aware of the needs of others.

Caring in the fullest way for a family takes a lot of time and energy. That brings us to another question, much discussed nowadays: 'Are you happy to be a mother at home?' My answer is, 'Yes, tremendously!' I feel it is a great privilege to have time to give to the children, to their friends, families and teachers.

Though I have no official status, I have several times had a part in shaping the thinking of the school or the thinking in the city. I simply obey that inner voice which tells you to write that letter or to make that phone call, even if you are nobody, just one of the silent majority or minority! Once I felt that the Catholics in our town needed help on an important issue. Myself a Protestant, I wrote a letter to our daily paper which was published. Later I heard that it had made the front page in a Catholic newspaper. I cannot do such things every day, but I find that while you are doing housework your mind is often free to think. My best thoughts often come with the song of the vacuum cleaner and in the to-and-fro of the iron!

Lucy who lives in France found that her bitterness towards her father was threatening her relationship towards her husband.

My parents were separated, then divorced when I was in my teens. I went to live with my father. I felt as if I had been torn in half. Life with my father, who remarried twice, left me with deep hurts. Little by little I discovered that this bitterness against him had poisoned my relationship with everybody, even with Daniel, my husband. Some change began to take place when I decided to forgive my father and to open my heart again to him. But the brightest beam of light did not come until the day when I found total healing of that bitterness, making the most painful events in my life my greatest asset in helping other people.

76

It happened through Daniel. He felt that these first changes which had happened in my life were real but that it was possible for me to find total freedom from the prison of the past. I did not want to think about it at first, but when he kept on about it I decided to look again at that very painful period of my life. It suddenly struck me that even if I had forgiven my father, I still had to ask him to forgive me for my feelings against him. I wrote him a letter and showed it to Daniel. He said, 'It is not very convincing. I can still read blame between the lines, as if you are saying, "If you had behaved differently then we would have been spared all the suffering." '

While I was writing the third draft, a curtain was swept aside in the very depths of my soul, unveiling the real truth: for the first time I felt that I needed to be forgiven for the cruel way I had barricaded my heart for years. I wept when I began to feel the loneliness of my father and my responsibility for it.

The letter went off. A few weeks later, after an agonising wait, I got a profoundly moving reply. In his letter he opened his heart to me and told me where he felt he had been to blame and apologised for his faults. A heavy load fell from my shoulders. After all these years I had a father again! After that, bitterness could still tempt me but it never had any hold on me again.

Daniel: One evening shortly after we were married Lucy told me, 'I love you very much, but from now on I want to live according to what I think God expects of me and not what you expect of me.' I should have been delighted but I was furious. I went to bed furious and the next morning I was still so angry I stayed upstairs when Lucy went down for breakfast.

Then in a time of listening to the inner voice I realised that something very important had happened between us the night before. Lucy had simply freed herself from the prison I had put her in, a prison which demanded from her certain behaviour to satisfy my ambition and pride. She had decided I was not going to be able to control her life any longer even if I did this unconsciously most of the time. It was not only that she wanted to get free, she was offering me the best security for our marriage and above all the best proof of love any husband could wish for.

'Where would you like me to change?' was the question a Frenchman asked his wife. This is her account of events:

I had always wanted to marry a gentleman farmer; and as the daughter of a Paris doctor my dream was to live in the country.

And that was exactly what happened—rather far away, perhaps, as we were in Morocco, but that made it all the more wonderful.

In 1912 my father-in-law had settled in Morocco, in Marrakesh, where he had started different enterprises, and it was to his 750-acre farm, twelve miles from the city, that Charles and I went to make our home.

There was a large garden, full of roses and geraniums; there were olive groves, orange, apricot and almond orchards—there were around ten thousand trees in all—and still lots of virgin land to develop. To take my baby out, I only had to rock his cradle under the spreading lemon tree, and later our three children made the most of this life close to nature.

I had to make a start at learning Arabic, if only to understand the farm girl who helped with the housework.

My days were quite full, and Charles sometimes criticised me for not being free to go with him more often into the plantations: it was invariably time to feed the baby or change his nappies. When he returned in the evening he dived into his precious newspapers while I kept to my sewing.

'Life in the country' wasn't quite matching up to the ideal I had dreamed of for our marriage.

In 1954 the situation in Morocco was becoming serious. On the one hand there was a campaign for independence and on the other the French Government was reluctant to let its protectorate go. Some friends told us about Caux, the Moral Re-Armament centre in Switzerland, where many solutions to political problems had begun to take shape. In the spring when we received a formal invitation to attend the summer conference there, we immediately decided to go.

At Caux we went to many meetings and met many people. Charles, in true French style, argued point by point. He was very well up in politics and held lots of opinions. I was not in the least interested in affairs of state, but I let him do the talking and didn't get involved. After all, wasn't a wife's role to keep peace in the home? I thought I had done quite well— I kept quiet on everything that might make my husband explode. So we rarely discussed things between ourselves.

Life at home hadn't turned out as I had hoped. But I had resigned myself to the fact that on earth you don't get the ideal and the best you can do is to learn to live together. There in Caux, for the first time, I came across the idea of 'changing', the hope that it is possible to become different.

In particular I remember a Brazilian couple. He was a keen member of his political party and used to spend every evening with his union making big speeches on individual liberty, while she, the self-sacrificing wife, waited cheerlessly at home and saw to the housework.

The Brazilian couple were very different from us in many ways—race, religion, education, life-style, background—but on a human level we were exactly the same. So when I saw the life in their faces I realised that if change had been possible for them, it could also be possible for us.

On our eighth day at Caux, Charles came and asked me this wonderful but bewildering question, 'Where would you like me to change?'

You can imagine what it means to a woman when her husband asks her something like that after six years of marriage. It was like a great window opening on to a clear sky. Charles didn't believe in God, and didn't accept this idea of listening to the inner voice. But he recognised that honesty, purity, unselfishness and love were necessary in politics and that it would be excellent if our leaders were more honest. He also admitted that everyone had a conscience and finally agreed to try the experiment of listening.

So there he was beside me, asking that question. It took my breath away. Not being a courageous person (while he boils over quite easily) I had always been afraid of making him angry. I used to suppress my own outraged feelings very often. Very moved, anxious not to be hard or to take advantage of him, I was at a loss for words.

Then a small incident came into my mind. It had happened six months earlier and had left me frustrated. 'Do you remember the day when I had read the newspaper to please you?' I asked. 'And I asked you some questions because I hadn't understood everything? Why did you tell me to go and jump in the lake instead of explaining things to me?'

'Yes, I remember it very well,' Charles answered seriously. 'I told you to get lost because you asked some thorny questions which I couldn't answer. It was easier to say you were stupid than to admit my ignorance. I am sorry.'

The cork of the champagne bottle had popped and the foam could freely overflow. For the first time the way was open for us to say everything to each other, without fear or quarrelling.

We walked down across the lawn to a seat. There, with the view before us, we opened our notebooks and we each made four long columns, one for each of the standards—absolute honesty, purity, unselfishness and love—and also a list of all the people whose lives were involved with ours, at the top he and I, then our parents, children, servants, workers, friends, enemies . . .

In silence, quite quickly, and in a surprising way we began to see where we had fallen short. I used to think myself so honest—I had never stolen or (hardly ever) cheated at school. But what about all those secret thoughts which, in the name of domestic peace, I took care not to reveal to Charles? Weren't they really dishonesty? And the dream picture I indulged in of that marvellous husband, which was my escape from the reality I found too hard? Wasn't that really impurity?

Charles discovered that his frankness with me often had a streak of cruelty in it, and was totally devoid of love.

I have a vivid memory of the urge that took hold of us, the freedom to say everything. How wholesome it was, and with it came the courage to be open about the most difficult things. It was the turning point of our life, the start of a complete trust between us. Our relationship was transformed. It began to lead us to take an entirely new interest in other people.

As, bit by bit, I was getting off my chest everything that had weighed on me and all the deceptions which kept us apart, and as Charles realised what his attitude had cost me, an awful discovery began to dawn on him: the colonial regime was right there in us.

Though we prided ourselves on being progressive and would publicly have dissociated ourselves from colonialism, here was this evil in us. Our relationship had been just like that between the French and the Moroccans. Charles was like the French who assumed authority to make decisions without asking the others' advice. I was like the Moroccans who kept quiet for fear of becoming worse off than before.

We returned to Morocco with a new sensitivity to human needs and a readiness to listen for the guidance of God.

Next spring, Morocco had an invasion of locusts. Thanks to the skill and devotion of a Moroccan engineer who was in charge of pest control, our farm and many others were saved from disaster. One day Charles had a thought which might seem simple and obvious, but in fact was far from it, at a time when French and Moroccans hardly met each other. He thought he should go and see his engineer in the Ministry of Agriculture and thank him for doing such an effective job.

Charles took the chance to tell him what he had learnt at Caux. He mentioned the four standards. This only increased the Moroccan's mistrust, for he had never met an 'unselfish' European settler and wondered what lay behind this move. However, he had been touched by our thanking him, as he told us later when we became very good friends. He had also made enquiries among our workers to know what they thought of Charles.

When he learnt from them that we had stopped having any wine or spirits in our home, he was intrigued and invited us to lunch. I must admit I did not feel too happy going to his home, as there had been demonstrations here and there against the French, but during the meal a real relationship of trust was born.

He wanted to know what it was that could transform the mentality of a French settler. A few weeks later he and Charles took the plane for Caux together. Upon their return to Morocco this engineer took very courageous action which led to the country getting its independence without bloodshed.*

For seventeen years we shared our home with another family, a father, mother and son.

Our neighbours used to wonder how we managed without coming to blows. They used to say, 'You mean, you even share the kitchen?' We lived as one family, we had all our meals together. Of course it was very economical, we only needed one vacuum cleaner, we had only one gas bill to pay, we also grew our own vegetables. We divided the house cleaning, each one had his or her task, including the menfolk.

We were free to be away from time to time because we have looked after each other's children, whenever this was necessary.

The three children learned to take corrective from the other adults in the home. They learned that they were not the centre of attention, that there was no room for moods or temper, that we all worked together to entertain the many people who came to our home and that each person who came in was to be treated as one of the family.

In a survey about living in communes I read that many break up because each woman has a definite ideal of how to bring up her child and finds it impossible to agree on a common way of practice.

We had the same experience—we were different personalities from different countries. We had different ideas about what the children should eat for instance. We found we had to make common rules about bedtimes when the children

---

* For full story see *The Lords of the Atlas* by Gavin Maxwell (Longmans, 1966).

were smaller, and about how much television they should watch and which programmes. We had to be frank with each other on all issues and then see together what was right. It may sound simple, but it only works if you have the same values and the same basic aim in life, otherwise one person is bound to dominate the others and there is dictatorship instead of freedom.

Paul should have the last word:

I grew up on the Canadian prairies in a home fashioned by a Scottish Baptist minister from the West Highlands and my English-born mother from Yorkshire.

One bitterly cold winter an influenza epidemic decimated town and countryside. Strong men and little children succumbed, sometimes very swiftly, to the virus and the subsequent pneumonia. Antibiotics were still to be developed.

My only sister, aged six, named after Edith Cavell, the English nurse who was shot for aiding the Allied soldiers in Belgium during the First World War, caught the infection. My mother nursed Edith as well as some of the neighbours who were too ill to help each other.

The night my sister's last strength crumbled I was asleep in my father's bed. My mother slept near her sick child. In the morning when I wakened my father said to me, 'Edith has gone to be with Jesus.' Her last words to Mother and Father were, 'I love Jesus.' That simple affirmation of faith in the reality of the Unseen assuaged the pain that ran too deep for words or tears.

A few days later at the memorial service held in our living-room, Ben, a big strong six-foot-two farmer, stood beside my father. At one point I saw him close his hand over my dad's.

It was in the family circle that I first learned that pain can be used to heal. The death of my sister created a deeper compassion in my parents, greater gentleness and a quiet patient strength.

Twenty-six years later Ben again stood beside my father and me when my mother left us, and seventeen years after that Ben stood beside me and my wife when we buried my father beside my mother and sister. It was in the family that I learned that true friendship is a prize beyond measure and lasts for life. It is based on give and not on get. And in the family I learned that suffering deepens and strengthens the soul like no other force.

In our family we often had our differences, but I was never allowed to be disagreeable for any length of time. Consequently we had no fights. My father and I did not always see eye to eye on my attitudes and opinions, which clashed with his most cherished beliefs, but I learned that it is possible to disagree, sometimes profoundly, without being disagreeable.

I learned about forgiveness, both to seek it when I had injured others and to give it fully when I felt I had been badly done by.

I learned that though I was free to choose, I was never free to avoid the consequences of my choices.

One day I brought home some tennis balls from a court near the primary school which I attended. When my parents found out, for the one and only time father's razor strap was applied to that part of the anatomy where he calculated it would do the greatest good with the least injury. I had to go to the school principal and tell him that I had taken the balls, which I was returning.

I learned that success was a hollow ambition and failure a false fear. Success in my parents' eyes was that, whatever the result, I had done my very best. And I learned in my home that selfish choices had far more serious consequences than failure. To achieve success and to avoid failure were motives centred on self. To be conscious of the cost of my choices on others made me aware of a selfishness for which I needed to apologise, to make restitution and to seek forgiveness from God and man. I found this to be the highway to inner freedom and discipline and to change.

In the home I learned how obedience opens the door to the highest wisdom. My will was often crossed. I cannot imagine any in my circle who would have crossed my will the way my parents did, for they were the only ones who cared selflessly enough to do it. To cross my will, sometimes with firmness, sometimes with humour, was one of the greatest things my parents did for me.

A neighbour saw me with other boys smoking dried leaves behind the barn. He told my father. Dad said to me, 'Why not invite your friends into the house and smoke there?' We were about eight years old at the time. The smoking session never took place. Somehow the fascination of imitating the grown-up habit was broken.

Both my parents believed in coming to the marriage altar with clean hands. This discipline marked our own marriage and it seems to us to be one of the foundation stones which give solidity and permanence to our family structure.

I learned too the priceless value and grace of humour in relationships. My father had a quiverful of Scottish stories with which he would regale the frequent visitors to our home and tell during the innumerable visits we made to other homes. To hear him and Ben swap stories was an hilarious experience to be cherished. I saw the care and selfessness that go into giving hospitality and how to receive hospitality.

My parents took me for the first time to hear a concert pianist. A new world dawned for me. For several days I was in a state of trance. It was an experience which shook me to the core. Mother herself was a good pianist and singer. I must have inherited some genes which vibrate to good music, but evidently not the genes required to produce it.

It was in the home that I was introduced to excellence in literature, beginning with the Bible and Shakespeare. It gave me a standard which has given me a great taste for the first class.

But the greatest treasure of all that my home made available to me was faith. I saw in my parents the reality of the Unseen. I saw lived out before me that God could and would provide for my needs, lead me, and forgive and change me if I asked Him. Their faith was real because it was practised. I could see it in the way they treated each other, their alertness to the needs of their neighbours, the effect on them of my sister's death. It was a faith that communicated, not because of their perfection but because of their honesty. Once they said to me that they had tried to be a model of family life for me to follow, but that a model to be effective has to be perfect. They were not perfect. They had their differences and misunderstandings between them, but they had never said so to me. One day they told me, 'If we were not honest with you when we were wrong, how could we expect you to be honest with us when you were wrong?'

I now try to put this lesson into practice with my children.

It was through our family life that I found the meaning of existence and the purpose of life: 'Seek first God's kingdom;' His will done in me and on earth; to try to please the Almighty in my thoughts, words and actions. Because my parents held to Christ's standards that right is right and wrong is wrong, I began to understand that I and no one else was responsible for my actions and circumstances and my future. An absolute sense of right and wrong leaves no room to blame the neighbours or bad luck or society. The responsibility for my life is my own.

My wife has the grace of being straightforward and honest with me and the children about her feelings of where we need to be different in order to do differently. She simply says it and leaves it, no nagging the point. Truth left to itself is a double-edged sword. If she would only nag, then I could quarrel with her on the details! But leaving me with the simple honest statement means that I have to resolve the matter in my own heart.

I have at times been absorbed by the importance of my own work, but I have learned to regard my children as being as important as any leader in politics, business or science. I know that it is easy for me to love my children, but difficult to be wise. I need the wisdom and insight that God's guidance brings.

We have learned in our family life that final authority is not with Dad or Mother or what the children want, but in what God wants, in what is right. We find that listening together to let the voice of truth in our hearts be heard is satisfying, authoritative and accurate for small decisions and for the tough ones, and that the inner voice gives the desire and freedom to obey the unenforceable. That voice speaks as clearly and wisely to a child as to an adult.

Years ago my younger daughter wrote some lines in her notebook. It moved me a lot to hear her idea of a father's role:

You are my child
You are your father's child
And I am your Father.
All fathers must take my place in life
and lead the world to unity
and make our fellow men brothers.

Fatherhood has made God's attitudes to His children clearer for me, for with all my limitations I am deeply interested in everything that touches the lives of my family—the quality of government they live under, the state of our society, the quality of education, the water they drink. Everything that touches their lives is of concern to me, and I cannot see my Heavenly Father being any less interested in every aspect of our welfare—political, economic and social—than I am in the welfare of my children. His interest is not limited to the state of my soul, vital as that is.

We have an aim in our family: the re-centring of nations and people on God's will and ways in every aspect of life. That aim gives perspective to the ordinary round, and a sense of direction and proportion to our living. This purpose is the cement that binds us together, heightens our values and aids us in our choices.

If there is an association of people better equipped than the family to pass on these rich gifts to the next generation and to our contemporaries, let's have it. But until then the family is the best school for acquiring the arts of living that has so far been devised. It could be called the Almighty's instrument for promoting the moral and spiritual evolution of the entire human family.